In Praise of *Gaining Traction*

As a professional who has focused on helping those who experience loss, and as a person who is in my third year of grieving the loss of my spouse, I recommend *Gaining Traction* without reservation. This book is an invaluable resource for anyone who has lost a life partner and particularly good for those who are beyond their first year after loss and think there is something wrong with them because they don't feel better. Counselors will also find this user-friendly volume a "must-have" reference.

> — **Janice Nadeau,** PhD FT, Psychologist,
> Marriage and Family Therapist

Vicki Panagotacos has an uncanny ability to tune in to her clients, which makes her one of the best grief practitioners I have known. She is eloquent and accurate in meeting each individual where they are emotionally — offering courage and hope for healing. Her caring, supportive and wise presence has translated well into her book, *Gaining Traction*. Read it and then pass it on to another you know and love.

> — **Lyn Prashant**, PhD FT, Somatic Grief Specialist

Panagotacos has listened well and thought clearly and compassionately about how to gently guide individuals back toward a full life after the death of their mate. Readers will feel Vicki's understanding of their complex experience and be enriched by her suggestions for imaginative thought and action. Excellent for clients and for pastors, therapists and counselors. I recommend this book to colleagues and friends with a full heart.

> — **Eric Greenleaf** PhD, Psychologist and Director,
> Milton H. Erickson Institute of the SF Bay Area

Vicki has been a gift to us here at Pathways Home Health and Hospice, and *Gaining Traction* has been the foundation of our 2nd year partner loss program she helped create. Her book provides inspiration and a much needed resource for those who are challenged to rebuild their lives without their loved ones. I am thrilled that others will have the benefit of her meaningful and helpful book.

— Chris Taich, MSW, LCSW, Director,
    Bereavement Services, Pathways Home Health and Hospice,
    Sunnyvale, CA

Gaining Traction offers the bereaved spouse/partner hope on their grief journey and practical insight into how to move forward in a healthy manner. The reader will appreciate the reflections of those having struggled in their first year of loss and their transformation after participating in the author's second year class.

— Brad Leary, LCSW, CT, Director, Social Services and
    Counseling, Hospice of the Valley, San Jose, CA

Vicki Panagotacos clearly understands the emotions and challenges a person faces when dealing with one's grief. She brings a wealth of knowledge and compassion to this book, and provides helpful tips and suggestions for navigating the future after partner loss.

— Dwight Wilson, CEO, Mission Hospice, San Mateo, CA

GAINING TRACTION

GAINING TRACTION

Starting Over
After the Death of Your Life Partner

Vicki Panagotacos, PhD FT

STEADY GUIDE PRESS

First Edition
Steady Guide Press
www.vickipanagotacos.com

© Copyright 2014 Vicki Panagotacos

ISBN: 978-0-9915805-0-7

LIBRARY OF CONGRESS CONTROL NUMBER:
2014937481

COVER DESIGN:
Sladjana Vasic

TEXT PRODUCTION:
D. Patrick Miller • Fearless Literary Services
www.fearlessbooks.com/Literary.html

TABLE OF CONTENTS

Acknowledgments ix

Introduction 1

CHAPTER 1
The Chapter That Can't Be Skipped 7

CHAPTER 2
Say Your Piece and Find Peace 15

CHAPTER 3
Same Sky, Different Vista 25

CHAPTER 4
Release Your Secret Sauce 39

CHAPTER 5
Spirit, with or without God on Your Team 45

CHAPTER 6
No Better Kickstart Than Being Petrified 53

CHAPTER 7
The Surprising Truth about Negative Chatter 59

CHAPTER 8
Guess What Else Is Running the Show? 69

CHAPTER 9
Change Your Body Language, Change Your Life 77

CHAPTER 10
Wired or Tired: Great Times to Act 83

CHAPTER 11
Ditch Willpower for the Power of Pretend 93

CHAPTER 12
Love Aside: "New Relationship" Facts and Figures 111

CHAPTER 13
Four Magic Questions You'll Thank Me for Asking 133

CHAPTER 14
On Track for a Life of Your Own 141

About the Author 149

Bibliography 151

Acknowledgments

I would like to thank the Directors of Bereavement at Hospice of the Valley in San Jose, California, and Pathways Home Health and Hospice in Sunnyvale, California, for supporting a second-year spousal loss program. I also want to thank the great interns and staff who helped me facilitate the monthly sessions over the years.

I feel a special gratitude toward my clients and the members of the second-year groups. You have been wonderful teachers. Thank you for your affection and kind words during our times together; thank you for your ongoing notes and emails keeping me abreast of how you are doing; and thank you for volunteering to review the manuscript.

Special thanks to the team who helped shepherd this project: Barbara McNichols, Patricia Nunn and Rose Marie Cleese for copy editing, Sladjana Vasic for cover design, Patrick Miller for interior layout and bringing the book to market, and Jim Leung and Vivian Shultz for their ongoing support. Lastly, I am indebted to content editor and marketing advisor, Nancy Gershman. Nancy provided tenacious focus, valuable feedback and stalwart support when I needed it most.

Introduction

The goal is not to get over the death. The goal is to reconcile with the unchangeable loss and integrate it into your life.

—Harold Ivan Smith

A S A ten-year-old child, I had a pet parakeet named Happy. I taught Happy to say several words, pluck a piece of cracker from between my lips on the fly, and land on one of my shoes for a ride. We had a regular routine and often performed for the family.

One day, a man was hired to steam the wallpaper from our dining room walls. As he put a huge metal plate to the wall, condensed water from the steam ran down his arms and onto the floor. From watching him, I understood why he was wearing rubber boots.

I remained fascinated by the whole process until I saw Happy fly past me and land on one of the man's boots. The ride didn't go as Happy expected. As the parakeet slipped off the wet boot, the man's next step ended Happy's life. Wailing, I ran into the dining room and picked up Happy's lifeless body from the wet floor.

I have no memory of the rest of the day. But the following day, my mother told me to put on my coat because we were going to buy a new bird. I was too numb to object.

I remember standing in front of the big cage of birds at Woolworth's and refusing to pick another bird. Finally, my mother asked if I thought it would be a good idea to buy a green parakeet this time instead of a blue one, and I nodded in agreement. Unwilling to give up Happy, I named the new bird Happy Two.

Not long after I watched my mother start her typical Saturday cleaning by unhooking the bird cage and heading for the back yard with Happy Two swinging wildly on his perch. I rushed to the kitchen window and standing on my tiptoes, I watched her rap the sides of the cage to loosen bird seed and feathers. What was she thinking? The bird was still in the cage and the bottom was gone!

Sure enough, within seconds, Happy Two took a nosedive down through the bottomless cage and flew into a nearby tree. My mother stood paralyzed, staring into the air, and then slowly turned to see me standing at the kitchen window.

I immediately joined her and together we shouted for Happy Two to come back, but as we called his name, I think we were both relieved that he was gone. Now we wouldn't have to pretend that Happy's death could be easily fixed.

Even though I had attended countless rural funerals and played under open caskets in parlors with other children as a toddler, Happy was mine. He belonged to me. Therefore his demise was a palpable rite of passage. I now understood that life would not be a string of untarnished pleasure and pretending not to be sad was hard work and useless. However, the most significant lesson was that in spite of the tragedy, I had the capacity to recover.

From childhood forward, loss brings each of us to sorrow's door and asks us to enter what Parker Palmer terms "the tragic gap"[1]— that place of tension between the dark down and in reality and the up and out possibility that something worthy will emerge.

Palmer acknowledges how difficult it is to stand off-balance in the tragic gap. Some of us don't understand its value and try to ignore the gap; some of us fear we will be consumed by it and try to escape into a busy calendar. Neither resolves our grief. Sooner or later we must mourn until we can gather our wits about us and decide it is time to come up and out into the world once again.

Seeking permission to come up and out

Years ago, I spent a week with the late Lou Tice, who founded the Pacific Institute. I was intrigued by his comments about how we are conditioned to depend upon an outside authority to give us permission to move forward.

Specifically, he spoke of how our educational system raises children to wait for permission before advancing. As adults, society often requires us to take an oath before we can be qualified to enter the military or become a policeman, fireman, physician, lawyer, or join certain organizations.

In this book, I encourage you to challenge the unconscious mindset that tells you that you are unqualified until you are told you are qualified by someone else. I urge you to not get caught up in seeking consensus from others. Instead I prod you to commence the process and remember that the line between being unqualified and qualified is not an entrance with a door and doorman but, rather, a porous state of mind to be explored. Count on the fact that as you read this book your head will clear, and you will get a grip on who you want to become.

How this book came about

For years I facilitated hospice grief support groups including spousal/partner loss. As the first-year partner loss groups ended, I was asked repeatedly about a second-year program. There wasn't one, but the more I thought about it, the more I realized that there should be. Yes, the first-year group had helped members work through their fresh grief, but the questions that began to surface at the end of the year had not been answered: What's going to happen to me? Do I settle for what little I have left? If not, how do I start over?

It was clear that Medicare's mandated year of bereavement support had not provided members with what they would need to move into the often more daunting second year after loss.

In 2001, the Director of Bereavement at Hospice of the Valley in San Jose, California, gave me the green light and a second-year class was posted in the newsletter. The following fall we had more people than we had chairs.

The class was designed to break the overwhelming task of starting over into manageable parts. As each session built upon the last, members came to understand what would happen if they did nothing. As the year progressed, the men and women relaxed into the process and started to define their options.

The material that I prepared for those partner loss classes has made its way into this book, including the probing questions and exercises I call TR·*ACTION*s. If you are inclined to skip over what may take a few minutes to complete, please don't. Those who have kept in touch with me over the years have said, almost without exception, that learning more about what motivated their thoughts and actions was critical in helping them manage their anxiety as they defined their future.

To help support your journey of discovery, I have also included the voices of many who have done the work by providing between-chapters sidebars of class members' comments.

It has been my privilege to watch hundreds of people from different economic and ethnic backgrounds lean into their discomfort, find the courage to stretch beyond what they thought they could tolerate, and blossom in ways they would never have predicted. It is my wish that this book will help you do the same.

Notes

1. Palmer, Parker (1999). An Active Life. San Francisco: Jossey-Bass. p. 66.

CHAPTER ONE

The Chapter That Can't Be Skipped

Grief and loss accumulate like possessions.
—Stefan Kanfer

Accepting loss as a constant in life

IF YOU have read any of the grief and loss literature, you have been reminded that your experience of loss started the day you moved from womb to breast, to bottle to glass. In fact, your childhood can be defined as a never-ending process of yearning for the familiar while eagerly opening up to the new. As you mature, however, your losses become more sobering and difficult to resolve.

Judith Viorst explains it well in her book, *Necessary Losses*, when she says,

> ...[W]e lose not only through death but also by leaving and being left, by changing and letting go and moving on. And our losses include not only our separations and departures from those we love, but our conscious and unconscious losses of romantic dreams, impossible expectations, illusions of freedom and power, illusions of safety and the loss of our own younger self.[1]

The loss of your mate is especially complex to manage because the two of you functioned as a couple for so long. You are not only dealing with the loss of your partner, but also the loss of your sense of self that was constructed through your interactions. If you are no longer someone's spouse or partner, then who are you?

Michael Miller[2] refers to the process of finding yourself as intimate terrorism. Your relationship has been blown apart, and you are left to sift through the emotional debris and extract the "I" from your vanishing "we." Understandably, your wounds are deep, and integrating the scar tissue takes some doing, as it should.

The incredible power of absence

As you struggle to redefine yourself as a single person, you may find that your partner's presence is actually heightened.

Author William Bridges contrasted the intense feeling of absence after his wife's death with how little he felt when she was alive and away for extended periods.

> Now her absence was palpable. It was a tangible fact that she wasn't there, and that fact made her emotional presence very powerful. It was less that I had feelings or thoughts about her than that I perceived her in absentia. It was as though there was always nearby, a shape cut out of space, an empty silhouette of nothingness shaped exactly like her.[3]

Bridges describes his continual attempts to reconnect as a time of feeling flimsy — a beautiful description of being without while learning to create a continuing bond.

The value of maintaining a continuing bond

It was once thought that people should strive to reach a definitive end to their grieving, often referred to as "closure." Research has since dispelled the concept as unrealistic and not even desirable. In fact, studies show that the most successful transitions take place when surviving partners maintain a bond with the deceased. It has also been determined that maintaining a continuing bond with the deceased does not detract from the success of a relationship with a new partner.[4]

One way to maintain a sense of continuity is to occasionally set aside some private time for looking at photographs, letters, cards, and small gifts the two of you exchanged. This quiet time will not only give you an opportunity to remember your loved one but — equally important — you can remember yourself as well. When there's suddenly no physical trace of your life partner, your own history can feel like it's been erased as well.[5]

Making a conscious decision to move forward

A few years ago, Father Gregory Boyle was interviewed by Terry Gross on National Public Radio's Fresh Air[6]. As I listened to this poignant interview, I found a parallel to what we do for another when we listen to someone for whom love has departed.

Boyle had been working with gang members in East Los Angeles for over 30 years. He buried more than 120 young people as a result of gang violence and witnessed the intense grief of family members mourning their murdered young men.

During the interview, Boyle emphasized that gang allegiance is driven by a need to feel connected to others. In an attempt to give these young people a sense of belonging to a larger world, Boyle tells the young men in detention that their lives are not taking place in a hole but in a tunnel. And they must trust that there is an opening at the end to the tunnel — one that will lead to a rewarding life and loving people.

Interestingly, Boyle doesn't see himself as a man of religion. Instead, he views himself as a man who "spends time listening to those for whom love has yet to arrive." In his willingness to listen, he believes he conveys more spiritual reality than if he were whispering religious doctrine.

Interviewer Terry Gross revealed that Boyle was diagnosed with leukemia the previous April but that it was in remission. She asked him if he prayed to live. Boyle answered that, centuries ago, desert monks prayed using the word "today," when they were despondent. In repeating "today," they remained present to access what was spiritually magnificent about the moment. Boyle said he also made "today" his constant prayer and found no need to pray for anything more.

Near the end of the interview, Boyle spoke of one particular young man and his dream. The boy had recounted how he was locked in a dark room with Boyle, who sat shining a flashlight beam onto the light switch on the wall. The young man knew that Boyle would never get up and flip the switch — that it would be up to him. Finally, the young man in the dream got up, walked over, and turned on the light. As he looked around the lighted room, he started to sob because it felt so much better than being in the dark.

We are not told exactly what took place in this young man's life, but a great deal of loss had to have transpired to lead him to his current circumstance. His dream, however, signaled a shift in the legacy of loss that he would pass to his children. By living in the light of "today," the young man came to understand that he could transcend the pain of his past and have a powerful legacy to carry forward.

What legacy of loss did you inherit and what will you pass on?

No child escapes inheriting positive and negative family legacies. Some stories are openly shared from adult to child, one generation to another. Some are never told because the emotional pain is intolerable and the story becomes taboo. Even though the unmentionable event may remain undefined, later generations nonetheless live with the "fallout" of the hidden legacy. In effect, they "remember" what they didn't experience — directly or in`directly.

Psychoanalyst and author Prophecy Coles talks in her book, *Uninvited Guests from Our Unremembered Past*, about intergenerational history: she says we must explore the uninvited guests we know so little about and in doing so, we can begin to "understand the history of our families' ideas."[7]

As you absorb what Coles is saying, I invite you to examine the ideas of loss that you inherited, especially if you are having difficulty resolving your grief. By investigating what took place ancestrally, you may see a family pattern. If so, is it a pattern you wish to adopt? Further, is it a pattern you wish to pass on to your loved ones?

I was not told of my family's repeated experiences with untimely death and unresolved grief over spouse and child loss until I was in my late 40s. Subsequently, I came to understand how the unresolved grief had negatively affected the attitudes and life strategies of three generations of women in my family. The point is not to tell a sad story. Rather it's to make you aware of how unresolved grief is passed on unconsciously and nonverbally via metaphor, tone of voice, and body language.

To help you understand the legacy of loss that you are currently transmitting to others, ask yourself these questions:

- How am I teaching others to view death and cope with emotional injury?

- Am I actively working to resolve my grief, or am I allowing it to manifest as callousness and self-protection?

- What legacy of loss do I want to leave behind? Would a worthy legacy be that, despite the anguish, a person can find the strength to grow in the shadow of loss and live a rich and fulfilling life?

TR·*ACTION*

As you move through the book, stop when you experience resistance. Ask yourself whether the resistance comes from everyday procrastination, fear, or a family legacy of moving away from risk. Gauge how the resistance will affect your future and, ultimately, the future of loved ones who are observing you.

Yes, life is messy. Yes, rebuilding your life is unsettling, uncomfortable, and infused with fear. And, because you are human, you will continue to feel inadequate — often. But I challenge you to accept the fact that you are overestimating what threatens your sense of emotional safety.

You are standing in the middle of an intersection. For now, pick a direction, any direction, so that you can yield to the truth: you are more resilient and capable than you think.

*Fran's reflections on life after the death
of her husband from a heart attack*

After Bill died, I didn't think I would ever feel settled again. I had children at home and so I buried my own needs. The biggest hurdle was accepting the fact that I needed help. It took me five years to get into counseling. Too long. By that time I was physically ill. It was difficult to accept that I wasn't weak and incapable because I needed help.

Much to my surprise, I have become an amazingly resourceful person and have embraced life with positive energy. When I look back over the past few years, I realize my mistake was in trying to schedule my grief between work and other responsibilities. I treated it like an activity versus a state of mind that needed attention.

Notes

1. Viorst, Judith (1998). *Necessary Losses.* New York: Free Press.
2. Miller, Michael (1996) *Intimate Terrorism.* New York: W. W. Norton.
3. Bridges, William (2001). *The Way of Transition: Embracing life's most difficult moments.* Da Capo Press.
4. Klass, D., Silverman, P. R., and Nickeman, S. (1996). *Continuing Bonds.* Washington, D.C.: Taylor and Francis.
5. Belk, R. W. (1988). *Possessions and the extended self.* JOURNAL OF CONSUMER RESEARCH, 15, 139–168.
6. National Public Radio: 2010 Program: Fresh Air interview with Father Gregory Boyle.
7. Coles, Prophecy. (2011) *Uninvited Guests from Our Unremembered Past: an exploration of the unconscious transmission of trauma across the generations.* London: Karnac Books.

SIGNS THAT TELL YOU THAT YOU SHOULD SEEK OUTSIDE SUPPORT

Whatever your age, there are times when it is wise to ask for help. If any of the following applies to you or your loved ones, take action. Make an appointment for counseling at your hospice, call your physician for a referral, or arrange to meet with your pastor or rabbi.

– You are having trouble functioning on a daily basis.

– You view life as hopeless.

– You can't get out of bed in the morning.

– You reject all invitations.

– You never leave the house unless it's an emergency.

– You overeat, over-drink, or abuse prescription drugs.

– You have panic attacks on a regular basis.

– You don't sleep for days on end.

– Your children are acting out, getting poor grades, or not talking to you

CHAPTER TWO

Say Your Piece and Find Peace

Simple awareness can be curative.

—Fritz Perls

JUST AS a room needs a good cleaning to remove what has accumulated, it is wise to examine unpleasant events and emotions that cling to the corners of your mind regarding your relationship with the deceased. Negative thoughts and emotions are common, but many of us have been convinced that it is wrong to feel them. In my opinion, the greatest misunderstanding to evolve from the *positive thinking movement* is that it is wrong for a person to feel anything other than grateful and glad. To the contrary, it is healthy to both accept and explore whatever emotion you are feeling.

Coping with feelings of self-blame and guilt

If you were your partner's primary caregiver, you most likely lived in a constant state of emotional and physical exhaustion with little time to take care of your own needs. In spite of your dedication, stamina, and tolerance, you would be the exception if you didn't also experience occasional anger and resentment — and guilt. You might also feel that you could have prevented your partner's death and regret not having been more assertive while your partner was alive.

TR·*ACTION*

If you find yourself caught up in self-blame and guilt, consider whether you would judge a friend as harshly as you are now judging yourself. If the answer is no, try to make peace with what you did well. If the guilt persists, ask yourself whether you are using your guilt as a way of keeping the relationship alive.

Dealing with blame from family and friends

As the death of a loved one approaches, family and close friends often feel overwhelmed and helpless. In frustration, they may unconsciously search for someone to blame for the circumstances they can't tolerate — and you may be the person they have decided to blame.

TR·*ACTION*

If you have been criticized or blamed for something another thinks you should or shouldn't have done around the time of death, ask yourself:

- What reason might they have for blaming me?
- Could their comments be more about themselves than about me?
- Was my reaction to their comments over the top because I was so overwhelmed?
- Would it be wise for me to give them the benefit of the doubt?

Feeling anger during the time of death

Kathy was a client of mine who felt tremendous anger because she and her husband had not experienced a "Hollywood death." I had never heard of a "Hollywood death" and asked her what she meant. Kathy described a scene in which the dying individual expresses his love for the other as he takes his last breath and quietly slips from the arms of his surviving spouse. After a brief pause, Kathy exclaimed, "I now feel foolish for assuming he ever loved me!" When she saw my quizzical expression, she added, "Well, he must not have loved me; why else would he turn away from me the last few days?"

As the session continued, she also told me about an argument she had with her sister-in-law the week before the death and confessed to me, "I don't care if we ever speak again!" Finally the tears came, and as she wept she said, "I feel gypped because his death didn't bring everyone together like it was supposed to."

Now that I knew what a "Hollywood death" meant, I understood: we all want a storybook ending. But it is so often not the case.

Unfortunately no one had helped Kathy understand how much energy it takes for a person to die and, therefore, how necessary it is for the dying to turn away from the living as death approaches. After we talked about the dying process, I commented that Hollywood is just that: Hollywood, a romantic mythical world of unrealistic expectations that seldom matches reality.

Feeling anger after the death

When I ask group members if they have felt anger since their partners' deaths, it is not uncommon for someone to recoil and say, "How could I possibly be angry at my partner for dying? That sounds awful!"

I agree. Being angry *at* someone for dying does sound terrible, but the truth is this: few people escape feeling angry *because* of the death. Being angry *because* your loved one has died is a rational response due to the facts that 1) you had no choice in the matter, 2) your life is shattered, and 3) you are suddenly faced with new responsibilities.

The following are a few comments I hear when clients speak honestly:

- "I'm angry because Jim is not here to help me do _____."
- "I'm angry because Sue isn't here to go with me to _____."
- "I'm angry because I didn't want _____, and now Bill isn't here to take care of it."
- "I'm angry because Karen isn't here to give me advice."
- "I'm angry because I am alone. I don't deserve this!"
- "I'm angry because I have to _____, and I feel so stupid and helpless."

Sound familiar? If so, accept the feeling and sit with it. After the feeling or emotion has made its way around your mind, start a list of outside service people who can help you do what you can't, and make a list of people who can join you for activities you once shared with your partner.

When it IS appropriate to be angry at your partner

People tend to assume that grieving is easier for those who have been in difficult and often abusive relationships. They are relieved, right? Don't be so sure.

If you were in a relationship where psychological or physical abuse came from the deceased, you are, indeed, entitled to be angry *at* your partner. Being angry at them, however, doesn't mean that you won't mourn the loss.[1] On the contrary, survivors of abuse often mourn what they had hoped for and now know will never be. It is also common for them to mourn the years they have lost by staying in the relationship.

The good news is that a 2004 study[2] found that those individuals diagnosed with depression while their partner was alive became depression-free within 6 to 18 months after the loss. Clearly, whatever the earlier circumstance, the partner's death eventually opened the door to their feeling a sense of freedom.[2]

Painful memories can step in the way of a functional future

Even though your living relationship has ended, it may feel incomplete because of unresolved issues. John James and Russell Friedman developed a Relationship Graph in their book, *The Grief Recovery Handbook*[3], that has been used successfully by thousands to *complete* their relationships after a death. I have adapted and simplified the process for you in this chapter.

I suggest you read the chapter straight through to familiarize yourself with the exercise, and then take the next few weeks to capture your thoughts and memories as they surface. After you finish the book, return to this chapter and focus on the step-by-step process outlined below.

What you wish could have been different, better, or more

To determine what was left unsaid, James and Friedman suggest you consider what you wish had been *different, better, or more*. They point out that, even though you may have spent months caring for and talking with your partner, you most likely didn't tackle earlier unresolved issues. I believe the primary reason people don't speak about unresolved disputes and disappointments is because 1) they don't believe they can do it without being unkind, and 2) they don't realize how good both parties will feel after the issues are discussed and resolved. That being said it is not too late to work through your feelings and find peace.

TR·*ACTION*

When developing your list, specifically address the emotional pain you caused the other person as well as the pain your deceased loved one caused you. In addition, include what you wish you would have said and done, as well as what you would have liked your partner to have said and done, and then respond to each circumstance with a statement of apology, forgiveness, or relevant comment.

Apology: An apology is self-explanatory. If you find yourself hesitating, ask yourself if your need to be right is getting in the way of apologizing. Remember this is about *you* taking action.

Forgiveness: What did your partner do or not do, say or not say, that you wish they had? Remember, you are forgiving to free *yourself*, not your partner. Forgiveness is always appropriate when there is no hope of something being different or better. (Note: be prepared to give up being self-righteous.)

Significant Emotional Statement: Being verbally accountable does miraculous things for your soul. Upon reflection, you might think of some other things you want your deceased partner to know, such as:
- I wish I had (been/said/done) _____ more often.

- I wish that you had (been/said/done) _____more often.

- I wish I had not (been/said/done) _____as often.

- I wish you had not (been/said/done) _____as often.

The following suggestions from *The Grief Recovery Handbook* can be very helpful in conveying undelivered communications:
- Be spontaneous with your writing and don't edit or limit your

comments. Also don't worry about listing things in perfect chronological order.

- Stay with feelings. Concentrate on what brings feelings of deep remorse, anger, and regret. Remember this is not an intellectual exercise about who was right or wrong.

- Avoid making the other person a saint or a devil.

- Remember: a good relationship includes some negative events; a bad relationship includes some positive events.

- Don't think an event is too small to include — *small accumulates.*

- Consider talking to a counselor if there was a significant ongoing problem. A caring person can help you reconcile and heal deep, long-standing wounds.

Now that you have the general idea of what is involved, follow the instructions below:

- List your unresolved partnership incidents and/or behaviors as they come to mind.

- When finished, place a number to the left of each entry so you can reorder them chronologically. Don't be concerned about exact dates.

- Take a fresh piece of paper and list the incidents/behaviors in chronological order and write your apology, statement of forgiveness, or significant emotional statement underneath each incident or behavior.

TR·*ACTION*

Writing your completion (not farewell) letter
After creating your list of apologies, words of forgiveness, and other significant statements, write a letter to your loved one. A sample format follows:

Dear _____,
In reviewing my relationship with you,
I apologize for ...
I apologize for...
I apologize for..., etc.
I forgive you for ...
I forgive you for...
I forgive you for..., etc.
I want you to know that...
I want you to know that ...
I want you to know that..., etc.

Because I love you, I want to say goodbye to any memory of emotional pain that was not resolved between us. In apologizing, forgiving, and being honest about what I wish had been more, better, or different, I now feel free to move into my future.
Love, _____

James and Friedman suggest you do not 1) ask your deceased partner any questions, 2) include comments such as "we did our best," or 3) ask your deceased partner for forgiveness. Why not? Because this exercise is about *you* taking action.

Read the letter aloud to a photo of your loved one or at the grave-site. If you unravel emotionally, continue speaking. When you are finished, give yourself credit for being wise enough to understand the value of your effort. Saying what's needed to be said doesn't mean you will never be sad again, nor does it mean you will not remember unpleasant memories. But it does mean that you will be in a better frame of mind to build a new, healthy life for yourself.

Dave's reflections on life after the death of his wife from breast cancer:

It took three years to adjust to being without Carol. While initially I expected to remarry, I found I was satisfied being alone and didn't feel compelled to date. Finally, friends and family persuaded me to venture out. Much to my surprise, I met a woman through eharmony. com and we dated three years before marrying. We have a great life together. Yes, life, again, is good.

The group was a great help because I realized that I wasn't alone. In retrospect, I can see that by reestablishing my own life, my children were then able to move on with their lives.

Notes

1. Kosminsky, Phyllis (2007). *Getting Back to Life When Grief Won't Heal.* New York: McGraw Hill.
2. Bonanno, G. A., Wortman, C. B., and Nesse, R. M. (2004). Prospective patterns of resilience and maladjustment during widowhood. Changing Lives of Older Couples (CLOC) study. *Psychology and Aging,* 19(2), 260–271.
3. James, J. W., and Friedman, R. (2009). *The Grief Recovery Handbook.* 20th ed. New York: Harper Collins.

Getting Back to Sleep

Sleep was likely a problem after your loss, and it might remain a problem because you no longer expect to sleep well. It turns out that what we think also affects how we sleep. Those who awaken in the middle of the night and expect to fall back to sleep usually do, while those who wake up and don't expect to fall back to sleep often don't.[1]

Besides changing your mind about middle-of-the-night awakenings, here are additional guidelines for a good night's sleep:

- Do not spend a lot of time in bed when you are unable to sleep.
- Avoid napping during the day unless exhausted.
- If you do nap, limit it to 45 minutes and put the alarm across the room.
- Avoid nicotine and caffeine at the end of the day, as stimulants take hours to wear off.
- Stretch to release any physical tension.
- Take a warm shower.
- Have a small no-sugar snack; you might not be sleeping because you are actually hungry. Consider a slow-digesting, low-calorie, low-sugar protein snack such as cereal with milk, a piece of chicken, a spoonful of tuna, a hard-boiled egg, a handful of almonds, or a banana.
- Go to bed at the same time every night.
- Read a chapter or two of a good but not too stimulating book.
- Be sure the bedroom is cool and dark.
- If you are not tired after going to bed, get up and do something enjoyable for an hour and then go back to bed.

Remember, drinking alcohol can cause you to fall asleep, but it can also cause you to wake in the middle of the night, so watch out for how much you drink.

Note

1. Jacobs, G. D., Pace-Schott, E. F., Stickhold, R., and Otto, M. W. (2004). Cognitive behavior therapy and pharmacology for insomnia. *Arch Intern Med* 164: pp. 1888–96.

CHAPTER THREE

Same Sky, Different Vista

For behind all things lies something vaster; everything is but a path,
a portal, or a window opening on something more than itself.
—Antoine de Saint-Exupéry, *Wind, Sand, and Stars*

Shifting from "what was" to "what will be"

STROEBE AND SCHUT define grieving as a process of "oscillating between stepping back into yearning for the past, and stepping forward to construct a future."[1] Dominique Browning refers to this as a time of alternating between "holding on and hiding, and holding on and seeking."[2]

In any case, it involves a kind of rocking movement, similar to how you would free your car when one of your tires sinks deep into mud or snow. As you shift gears from reverse into forward, rocking back and forth, back and forth, back and forth, you finally gain traction and are out of the hole — only to realize that you have little idea of where you are going. However, the lack of a destination is often less uncomfortable than the fear that you are leaving your loved one behind.

A woman in class once commented, "There was a time when I couldn't imagine feeling alive again, and now I freak out when I realize I haven't thought of my partner for a couple of days." This response is not unusual; some people say they prefer the pain

25

of grief over the uneasiness and apprehension that comes from starting over. As frightening as an undefined future can feel, you have two choices: you can (1) sink your stake of grief deeper and live in the past, or (2) pull up the stake and transform it into a rudder that guides you forward.

The first choice allows your grief to define the rest of your life; the second requires you to actively participate in *who you are to become*. By choosing the second option, you are signing up for what psychologists Tedeschi and Calhoun refer to as *post-traumatic growth*[3] and Tom Attig calls *relearning the world*.[4] Both imply that you become a student rather than an authority.

Sue's plane ride

Sue, an engineer who was in my first-year grief support group, later joined the second-year program. A few months into the second year, she said she thought she might be slipping into depression because she had no sense of direction regarding her life.

She considered setting goals for herself but said, "I can't define goals if I don't know what I want." Sue then confided that she wasn't sure she even wanted to live, but with two beautiful daughters in their early 20s, such thoughts made her feel selfish and guilty. After our group meeting, I approached her. As we talked, she assured me her love and responsibility toward her daughters would keep her alive.

A few days later, she called saying she would not be attending our next month's session because she was flying cross-country to an artist's retreat. I was surprised but pleased that she had made plans.

Returning to the group the following month, Sue reported the retreat was "okay but not great," but the trip home was high drama. An hour or so from New York, the pilot made an announcement that wasn't the typical "due to mechanical problems, we're going to land in Kansas" update. Instead, he instructed the attendants to prepare the passengers for a crash. As Sue braced herself against the seat in front of her, she was stunned to feel an intense desire to live. Thankfully, the plane landed safely, and as our group ended for the year, I believed Sue was on her way.

Months later, she saw me privately, wanting me to help her develop more structure in her life. I laughed, saying she sounded like an engineer, and I loved hearing her laugh in return. A few weeks later Sue showed up with long scratches on both arms. When I commented on them, she said she was removing a long hedge of shrubs in front of her home — by herself. She had always hated what had been planted and decided it was time to dig them up and plant what she wanted. My inclination was to suggest that she get some help, but I thought better of it.

We had been working with the Four Questions outlined later in this book, and even though the shrubs had not been on any of Sue's lists, she was, indeed, coming to define what she wanted by figuring out what she *didn't* want. She was also metaphorically nurturing her post-traumatic growth by planting and nurturing a new hedge.

Committing to life and loving yourself

Permit me to share how Denise continued to enjoy a passion she had shared with her husband. Denise was a petite, proper woman who often spoke with the group of her loneliness and emotional fatigue. After the holidays, she told the class that she had done what I had suggested: she had gone dancing!

Her story started when her niece invited her to San Francisco for lunch at one of the large hotels. The restaurant was on the top floor of the hotel, and their lunch was delightful. As they entered the elevator to return to the lobby, Denise spotted a poster advertising dancing that evening in the penthouse restaurant. Saying nothing to her niece about the poster, she walked her to the front door and told her to go ahead, that she wanted to go back and stop by the women's room. Instead, she headed for the reservation desk, booked a room, and asked the concierge to reserve a table for her at 8:00 p.m. in the penthouse restaurant.

As Denise shared her story, she noticed the class members' stunned expressions and abruptly stopped talking. "Well, why not?," she countered. "The worst thing that could have happened is no one asks me to dance!" While everyone nodded in agreement, she went on to say how much she had enjoyed the city view while dining and that she had, indeed, danced with several different men.

Denise had managed to bridge wanting things to be one way while knowing it was time to consider another. Why not take a page from her book and face the initial discomfort of doing something on your own?

TR·*ACTION*

Making a commitment to live and love yourself is key to loving life and loving others. Therefore, I suggest you figure out what you like about yourself and what you like doing. What activities did you do because they were your partner's interests — but not yours? Are you still doing them? If so, why? Lastly, what did the two of you do together that you now miss? Is there a way that you could enjoy the activity now, either alone or with another?

Fitting your family into your future

If you have adult children and grandchildren, they have likely been attentive, loving, and concerned about you since your partner's death. In turn, you have been grateful for their presence. Without thinking, you may have started to live through their lives rather than reconstruct one of your own.

If so, reconsider for everyone's sake. Your children aren't likely to comment, but they may feel ambivalent about being solely responsible for your lifestyle and happiness.

As you become more independent, it is important to develop the "muscle" to wisely respond to any objections your family may have regarding the decisions you are making.

For example, if you want to travel abroad and your family doesn't think you should, consider what they have to say and then make up your own mind. If they think you shouldn't spend the money, ask them why not? It's your money.

If you have started to date and your grown children object, ask them why, consider their reasons, and then make your own decision. Remember, you are teaching them by example how to survive the death of a life companion.

Forget goal-setting for now

As you move into the second year after your loss, you may, like Sue, think it's time to set a few goals. Instead I suggest you open your focus rather than narrow it.

Dan Siegel in *Mindsight*[5] says that we often live like we are walking at night through a major city with a flashlight beam directed straight ahead. We can clearly see what is illuminated; however, if we turn the flashlight off and give our eyes time to adjust, our vision widens. What do we find? *The world is much bigger than we ever imagined.* Why not let your eyesight adjust so you can capture what is softly illuminated in your peripheral vision?

Another reason to delay goal setting is to make sure you are drawn to your interests and not someone else's! Your earlier life goals may have unwittingly come from your family and, therefore, you could have worked hard to fulfill someone else's idea of a meaningful life. Stop. It's time to detach from others' influences so you can discover and follow your own interests.

In her book, *The Power of Mindful Thinking*[6], Harvard University researcher Ellen Langer offers another reason for not setting goals: they cause you to delay gratification. Considering what you've been through, do you really want to delay feeling better?

A key component to feeling better about today, as well as tomorrow, is to learn about what is *possible*. Langer warns that most of us don't have a clue as to how to do this because we have relied upon top-down and bottom-up methods of learning our entire life. The good news is there is a much better and more effective way to learn, and once you get the hang of it, you will never turn back.

Langer describes the three ways of learning thus:

- **Top-Down:** you rely on being told, what educator Alistair Smith calls the *swallow and spit method* of learning.[7]
- **Bottom-Up:** you rely on direct experience.
- **Sideways:** you approach experience "on the slant," which requires you to become aware of what is happening around you versus mindlessly walking past it.

When you were a child, how many times did someone say, "You aren't paying attention. Stop daydreaming!" The message was clear: stop being distracted and focus on one thing at the expense of everything else. But you were paying attention, weren't you? You were giving your attention to what interested you *at that moment*. Indeed, you were learning "on the slant" or "sideways."

If you are a person who needs to have a goal in mind, why not make it a general one such as "I will notice what is unfolding around me." If this sounds good for you, Langer's concept of sideways learning will be invaluable.

TR·*ACTION*

Let's explore a few examples of learning on the slant:

- You are invited to an art exhibit, a church service, a baseball game, or a continuing education course. You have no interest in art, church, or learning anything new. What is the upside of going anyway? What could happen if you expose yourself to what you don't think you'll enjoy?

- You decide to go on a tour of New England. Your partner always did the trip planning, and you simply don't know where to begin. Finally you buck up and approach the planning as a necessary evil — to be endured and completed quickly. But why delay your enjoyment until you are in New England? God forbid, you catch the flu the day before your departure or a hurricane closes the airport for days.

  If you allow yourself to become childlike and distracted, you are more likely to engage people at the library, lunch with people who have taken the trip (which could kick-start another activity later), and befriend a local travel agent (and end up attending his or her monthly travel club meetings).

- You are invited to a party and decline because another single person has been invited. Why? You are not ready to date and even if you were, you would never agree to be fixed up. Is it a good idea to say no? What could happen if you said "Yes," regardless of how you feel about the person, dating, or being fixed up?

  · You might find the person more interesting than you expected.
  · You might meet someone you do find interesting.
  · You might meet a new employer, a book/garden/bridge

club friend, or a hiking/walking/traveling connection.

By approaching activities sideways, you are open to unexpected pleasure. By shifting your focus from what is missing or wrong, you participate in what is present and right. By not insisting on knowing what happens next, you turn off the flashlight so you can see what is around you.

In *Vital Lies, Simple Truths*, Daniel Goleman speaks to how we fail to notice:

> *The range of what we see and do is limited by what we fail to notice, and because we fail to notice that we fail to notice, there is little we can do to change until we notice how failing to notice shapes our thoughts and deeds.*[8]

What will stop you from learning sideways?

The only thing that will trump your ability to learn sideways is your *refusal to feel fear*. Fear and anxiety are addressed in Chapter Five, but let's take a moment here to revisit what was probably the most fearful time in your life: the death of your companion.

Whether your loved one died unexpectedly or was ill for some time, you had no choice but to overcome intense fear and anxiety. Given different circumstances, you might have turned away, but you didn't. If your mate was ill, you gave the only thing you could give: your undivided attention to what was going on in the moment — in spite of your fear.

Why not use this well-earned, bottom-up learning experience to face your fear of reconnecting to the outside world? Why wait to offer others your undefended presence?

Susannah Conway says in *This I Know: Notes on Unraveling the Heart*, "Somewhere underneath the panic...hiding among the fear of failure, I knew it was time to move on...that by continuing to live in my cave, I'd never regrow that final layer of skin to cover my new bones."[9]

Ah... new bones...

When I read Conway's words, "new bones," I remembered a passage in a book called *Shambhala: The Sacred Path of the Warrior*[10] in which Chogyam Trungpa compares the birthing of a warrior to the process of a reindeer growing horns. At first, the horns are very soft, almost rubbery, just sloppy growths filled with blood. But with time, they grow stronger and develop into antlers.

A case could be made that you too are metaphorically walking around with tender, invisible, rubbery horns. If you could see them, they would not look like much. But as your fresh horns lose their soft, fine hair and become real antlers, it will dawn on you that they are *part of your becoming* — well-earned and beautiful.

TR·*ACTION*

Go to the drugstore or office supply outlet and buy multiple packets of Post-its®. Place a packet by the phone, the TV, the nightstand, in your purse, and in the car. Each time you think, read, or hear something that sounds interesting, write a word or phrase about it on a Post-it®. It could be join the library, set up an Amazon account, go to the movies, join a choir, attend a speaker's series, go bowling or horseback riding, take a class in painting or poetry, write in a journal — on and on and on. Get a haircut, buy a pair of jeans, attend a new church — on and on and on. Dine with friends once a month — on and on and on.

You might say, "I can keep the things I want to do in my head." You can't; it won't happen. That is why it's important to keep a Post-it® packet within arm's reach.

As you write on your Post-its®, peel them off and stick your future onto your closet door. If you run out of room on the door, buy a spiral notebook and stick the Post-it®s on its pages. If you want to immediately follow through with what you've written, do so, but don't toss the Post-it® notes. We are going to use them later.

Tell me again: why write down my thoughts?
Research[11] has shown that writing something down strengthens your neural pathways, causing your mind to start to "grapple with issues," increasing the odds that you will act on what you wrote.[12] One research study[13] showed that *before* writing, a certain amount of evaluating, ordering, and refining of ideas takes place, which causes the ideas to move from the abstract to the real.

Does this *on-going* Post-it® task still sound like it's too much trouble? Consider what business philosopher Jim Rohn said: "I find it fascinating that most people plan their vacations with better care than they plan their lives. Perhaps it's because escape is easier than change."

If you don't follow through with the Post-it® notes, it could be a sign that you aren't likely to follow through with getting what you would want and need from life. If there is a ring of truth to that last statement, I suggest you have nothing to lose and much to gain. So, please indulge me and buy those Post-it® packs *now*.

TR·*ACTION*

Do something different each day for the next month. For example, every morning before you throw back the covers and get out of bed, do the following stretches:

- Fold your arms and put them over your head while you

lengthen your legs as long as possible.

- Bend your knees, wrap your arms around your bent legs, and pull them to your chest. Leaving your knees bent, extend your arms out to the side and swing your bent knees to the right until they rest on the mattress for a couple of minutes. (If your left shoulder comes up a bit, that's okay.) Rest in this position. Then swing your bent legs over to the left until they touch the mattress and again rest in place.

- Unwind, curl up into a ball, and with your eyes closed, think of *one thing you are going to do differently today.*

  - Brush your teeth with your non-dominant hand.
  - Take a different route to a destination; do the same on your return.
  - Go to a supermarket you have never been to before. The goal is to experience the discomfort that comes from not knowing where a product is in the store.
  - If you usually wash your car yourself, go to a car wash (or vice versa).
  - Go to a movie by yourself and sit in the middle of the theater.
  - If you clean the entire house on Saturday, divide it up: clean the bathroom on Monday, the kitchen on Tuesday, the laundry room on Wednesday, and so on; and do something unusual on Saturday.
  - If you seldom smile, smile while drinking your first cup of coffee. If anyone sees you smiling, who cares?
  - If you resist writing letters, write one to someone — now.
  - If you rarely initiate a call to a friend, do so — now.
  - If you always feel obligated to clean and cook when inviting

someone over, don't touch a dust rag, bring in takeout, and don't apologize *ever again.*

For the next month, do one routine thing each day in a non-routine manner. The objective is to *become comfortable with discomfort* by stretching both your mind and body.

Sally's reflections on life after the death of her husband from cancer:

After Peter died, I never expected to feel whole again. I was stunned by how much anger I felt. It was tough being the only adult in the family with total responsibility for the finances. It was also difficult to always subordinate my own feelings in favor of my children's needs.

After the first year, I sold our home, bought a new one, and started to work. These decisions forced me to prove that I could handle responsibility. While my job gave me a sense of purpose, it took two years to regain any enthusiasm for life.

Learning to use the "Post-its" helped me to move forward with what I wanted versus what someone else might want. Today I am a strong independent woman, and I'm interested in growing personally and professionally. After four years on my own, I feel capable of being in another relationship because I have a healthier perspective.

Notes

1. Stroebe, M., and Schut, H. The dual process model of coping with bereavement: rationale and description. *Death Studies*, 1999. Vol 23:3.
2. Browning, Dominique (2002). *Around the House and in the Garden: a memoir of heartbreak, healing and home improvement.* New York:

Scribner.

3. Tedeschi, R., and Calhoun, L. (2004). Posttraumatic growth: Conceptual foundations and empirical evidence. *Psychological Inquiry*, 15:1, pp 1–18.

4. Attig, Tom (2010). *How We Grieve: Relearning the world.* New York: Oxford University Press.

5. Siegel, Dan (2010). *Mindsight: the new science of personal transformation.* New York: Bantam Books.

6. Langer, Helen (1998). *The Power of Mindful Thinking.* Cambridge, MA: DeCapo Press.

7. Smith, Alistair. Do Lecture. http://www.dolectures.com/lectures/why-we-need-to-change-how-we-learn/.

8. Goleman, Daniel (1985). *Vital Lies, Simple Truths.* New York: Simon & Schuster, p. 24. (Note: often attributed in error to R. D. Laing).

9. Conway, Susannah (2012). *This I Know: notes on unraveling the heart.* Guilford: Globe Pequot Press.

10. Trungpa, Chogyam (1978). *Shambhala: The Sacred Path of the Warrior.* Boston: Shambhala Publications.

11. Banikowsky, A. K. (1999). Strategies to enhance memory based on brain-research. Retrieved from http://sc-boces.org/english/IMC/Focus/Memory _strategies2.pdf.

12. Mangen, A. (2011). Digitizing literacy: reflections on the haptics of writing. *Advances In Haptics.* Retrieved from http://www.sciencedaily.com/releases/2011/01/110119095458.htm and http://www.uis.no/news/article29782-50.html.

13. Indrisano, R., and Paratore, J. R., (2005). *Learning to Write, Writing to Learn: Theory and Research in Practice* (No. 576-846). Newark, NJ: Intl Reading Assn., p. 91.

CHAPTER FOUR

Release Your Secret Sauce

Meaning makes a great many things endurable —
perhaps everything.
— Carl Jung, *Memories, Dreams, Reflections*

W HEN people share how their partner's death propelled them to create a new life, their notes and emails are filled with such comments as:

"I would never have known I had the strength to..."

"I would never have thought I had the talent for..."

"I would never have embarked on [a certain project, goal, activity, or passion]..."

"... if it hadn't been for the death of my partner."

Even though their partner had died, they realized they had not lost everything, nor were they any less worthwhile or lovable. To the contrary, the death had forced them to investigate underlying gifts and resources and pursue interests they would have ignored had the death not occurred.

Human beings are "meaning makers"

Viktor Frankl, best-known for his classic book, *Man's Search for Meaning*,[1] created a Viennese school of psychotherapy called

39

Logotherapy, which focuses on the future rather than the past. The term derives from the word *logos*, the Greek word for "meaning." Logotherapy's premise is that *life has meaning under all circumstances including tragedy.*

According to Frankl[2] each of us has a *will to meaning* that precedes our will to happiness. When we are able to use meaning as our frame of reference, we become fulfilled and ultimately experience happiness. Jungian psychologist James Hollis supports Frankl's premise in his book, *Swamplands of the Soul*:

> *During our lifetime we move from our fantasy of permanent happiness to the knowledge that we can live without happiness, but not without meaning; therefore we are required to continually reimagine ourselves in order to live in the present.*[3]

In *Finding Meaning in the Second Half of Life*, Hollis describes what comes from satisfying our soul's need for meaning. He quotes from the Gospel of Thomas: "If you bring forth what is within you, what you bring forth will save you." According to Hollis, this means that "the greatest freedom is found, paradoxically, in the surrender to that which seeks fuller expression through us — that which we are called to contribute and share with others and the world."[4]

Hollis also reminds us of what was touched on earlier and is addressed again later: few of us give ourselves permission to "bring forth what is within" because we are too busy living our family's expectations. Consider interrupting the need to please your family, and focus on pleasing yourself. Concentrate on what will add meaning and purpose to your life — and ignore what won't.

Parker Palmer, the respected teacher, creator of the *Circle of Trust*, and author of many books including *The Active Life*, says:

... every human being is born with some sort of gift, an inclination or an instinct that can become a full-blown mastery. We may not see our gift for what it is; or we may not choose to accept it and its consequences for our lives; or we may claim it but not be willing to nurture it. Regardless it is still the gift that is ours.[5]

Palmer asks us to separate our gifts from our acquired skills, reminding us that not all of our skills have been developed around our strengths. Isn't that so true? I once heard someone say we don't become tired when we are using our gifts, but we can become exhausted when using our skills.

TR·*ACTION*

What gifts do you possess that connect you to *who you are* rather than *what you do*?

List your gifts in one column and your acquired skills in the second column. When finished, consider which of them you are using at work, in your relationships, and in your community? Also ask yourself: if you are not using your gifts, why not?

TR·*ACTION*

While you are focused on your essence, write a scenario about *what your life would include if you could snap your fingers and have what you want,* **with no constraints,** such as monetary cost or your perception of what is age-appropriate. Give yourself permission to be outrageous. Write quickly and, for heaven's sake, don't consider whether you think you deserve it or not! When you finish, keep your "imaginary life with no constraints" for future reference.

*Mary's reflections on life after the death
of her husband from cancer:*

After Carl's death I had a hard time coping with the emptiness, and I couldn't accept that he was really gone. Reality set in quickly, however, because I had to step up and make major decisions regarding our business.

I still remember the first time I uttered the words, "I had fun." My brother asked me how my daughter's marathon had gone and I said, "Bill, I had fun!" I could barely believe that I was saying the word, "fun." It was a crazy, proud feeling — knowing that I could have fun again.

I was always good at getting people together on the spur of the moment to do something crazy and fun, but my husband preferred for me to remain reserved and plan everything in advance. I have to admit that it is nice to act the way I want to act. If I feel spontaneous and silly, I act that way.

The grief group was a lifesaver. If it weren't for that group, I am not sure I would have made as many wonderful new friends. Now? I still occasionally tear up, but I'm stronger, and I know God continues to guide my life journey.

Notes

1. Frankl, Victor (1959). *Man's Search for Meaning.* New York: Meridian/ Plume.
2. Frankl, Victor (1988). *Will to Meaning,* New York: Beacon Press.
3. Hollis, James (1996). *Swamplands of the Soul.* London: Inner City Books. p. 142.
4. Hollis, James (2006). *Finding Meaning in the Second Half of Life.* New York: Gotham. p. 12.
5. Palmer, Parker (1999). *The Active Life.* San Francisco: Jossey-Bass. p. 66.

Meditation

Meditation has been historically framed as a religious practice; however, I'd like to introduce the concept of meditation as a life tool outside of the religious context.

Mindfulness-Based Stress Reduction (MBSR) is an effective form of meditation with decades of evidence-based research behind it, most of it compiled by Jon Kabat-Zinn at the Massachusetts General Medical Center in Boston. Study after study shows significant decreases in everything from physical pain to emotional anxiety to depression after a mere eight weeks of doing MBSR meditation.

The August 2012 issue of Brain, Behavior and Immunity reported on UCLA research involving 40 adults aged 55 through 85.[1] Half the group attended eight two-hour weekly MBSR meetings and a one-day retreat. They also committed to a 30-minute daily meditation. The control group did not meditate. Those who meditated reported reduced feelings of loneliness. More than that, their blood tests showed a significant drop in the expression of inflammatory genes linked to heart disease, diabetes, Alzheimer's, stroke, and cancer.

Practically speaking, it is not easy for Westerners to sit in silence, but that is the beauty of MBSR. It provides a series of guided prompts that keeps you anchored in the present moment and away from ruminating over the past or an uncertain future. (If you are interested in having an audio copy of the MBSR meditation, it is available for a reasonable price on my website: www.TalkingGrief.com.) I also highly recommend *Full Catastrophe Living*,[2] even if you are not interested in meditating.

The following are a few alternatives to MBSR:

- Moving meditation: You can meditate while eating, walking, driving, or taking a shower. The point is to be aware of what you are thinking, feeling, smelling, tasting, or touching at the moment.
- Stop meditation: Several times a day, stop everything you are doing and become aware of your visual surroundings, sounds, and smells. Also be aware of where your body is making contact with your clothes, a chair, or the floor.
- In-bed meditation: Allow your awareness to move from the top of your head to your feet, breathing into any discomfort you might feel. Then shift your focus to parts of your body that you are unaware of — your earlobes, the back of your knees, your elbows, your ankles, the tops of your toes, or your fingertips.

Notes

1. Creswell, J. D., Irwin, M. R., et al. (2012). Mindfulness-based stress reduction training reduces loneliness and pro-inflammatory gene expression in older adults: A small randomized controlled trial. *Brain, Behavior, and Immunity*. doi:10.1016/j.bbi.2012.07.006.
2. Kabat-Zinn, Jon (1990). *Full Catastrophe Living*. New York: Delta Bantam Dell.

CHAPTER FIVE

Spirit, with or without God on Your Team

To everything there is a season, and a time and purpose
under heaven; a time to weep, and a time to laugh,
a time to mourn, and a time to dance.

— Ecclesiastes 3:1

I T WOULD take an entire book to explore how religion does
or does not influence a person's life after the death of a loved
one. Some individuals maintain their faith uninterrupted;
others find their faith shattered (especially if their partner dies
young and unexpectedly or after a long-suffering protracted
illness); still others feel a need to redefine their faith. Some have
no religious affiliation yet maintain a strong sense of spirituality
and, lastly, there are others who experience neither a religious or
spiritual connection.

Faith uninterrupted

Religious beliefs not only provide comfort but also a sense of
grounding for those who have historically found solace in their
faith. Many individuals include God and/or Jesus as close friends
with whom they talk on a regular basis.

Research[1] conducted by social psychologist Lee Kirkpatrick
and colleagues at the College of William and Mary found that
the more personal the bereaved's relationship with God is, the less

lonely they are — regardless of the other forms of support they receive.

Faith abandoned and then reclaimed

When people lose their lifelong faith in God due to the death of a loved one, they seldom realize they are simultaneously grieving the loss of their loved one *and* the loss of their faith. As they move through this dual crisis and their emotions stabilize, many return to their faith.

Psychotherapist Ashley Davis Bush tells of a Christian woman who lost her faith in God after the death of her husband and was left with nothing but questions. Instead of walking away entirely, she enrolled in a graduate seminary program to find answers. During an Easter Sunday sermon, the university pastor quoted Christ saying, "My God, my God, why have you abandoned me on the cross?" When the widow heard those words, something shifted for her: Christ's experience of feeling alone and abandoned became a companion experience to hers, which meant she was not really alone at all. Instead, she realized she was being "called to withstand, not understand."[2]

Faith abandoned and redefined

I recently watched a video of the 2012 Chautauqua conversation between Roger Rosenblatt, an essayist and practicing Jew, and Bishop John Spong, a retired Episcopalian bishop who has written extensively about religious doctrine. Rosenblatt's daughter had died five years earlier and in the interim he had written two books, *Making Toast*[3] and *Kayak Morning*[4] about his experience of moving into his daughter's home to help raise her small children while engulfed in his own grief.

Rosenblatt realized he had a secret agreement with his God that went something like this: "I'll be good and you'll do something for me." But when asked to explain God to another, his public version was: "The Deity sets life in motion and then says 'I wish you the best.'"

Rosenblatt admitted that he had lost his faith after his daughter's death but in "crawling back to it," he realized that his once-public definition had become his personal one as well. Now he thought God would qualify his earlier statement with, "I weep for the life that you have and that's all I can do — and possibly that is all I choose to do."

The bishop said he understood Rosenblatt's predicament. That is, if you define God as the supernatural being with the power to intervene, then God either becomes *malevolent* when he doesn't intervene or *impotent* because he can't intervene.

Nonetheless, Spong acknowledged that "our human experience seems to constantly drive us to try to define the word 'God' but because human rationale is our only tool, God too often becomes unbelievable." He went on to say that "people continually ask me to define or explain God, and I wonder why they think that anyone can do that." Instead, Spong said he felt only qualified to share his *experience* of the transcendent and his belief that prayer is something one lives, not something one does.

Rabbi David Wolpe traces his experience of being a "proud atheist" to returning to his faith and becoming a rabbi in his book, *Why Faith Matters*[5]. Shortly after accepting a position in Los Angeles, his wife was diagnosed with cancer at age 31. Four years later, he was scheduled for surgery for a brain lesion that had an 85 percent chance of being cancerous (but thankfully wasn't). Three years later, he was diagnosed with non-Hodgkin's lymphoma. When he found himself asking "why me?" he realized that seldom did anyone come to his office and say, "Rabbi, I live in the wealthiest country in the world and have never gone hungry

— why me?" or "You know my parents were good kind people and treated me with love — why me?"

"Obviously," Wolpe observed, "we seem to accept our blessings as our due, while difficulties in life cause us to rail against the injustices of the world."[6]

As both his and his wife's cancers went into remission, he came to understand that accepting the world as unfair should not lead to a conviction that there is no God, and that the "essential question of life [is] not why does this happen, which we can never fully know, but how do we create something powerful and lasting from our wounds."[7]

In the anthology *Loss of the Assumptive World*, Kenneth Doka acknowledges that "one of the most significant tasks in grief is for the living partner to redefine his or her religious belief in terms of whether the death was fair."[8] In his chapter entitled "How Could God?," Doka quotes C.S. Lewis from his book, *A Grief Observed*: "Not that I think I am in much danger of ceasing to believe in God. The real danger is of coming to believe such dreadful things about Him."[9]

Doka notes that when challenged, Lewis did not turn away from God — but accepted that his faith now "included a deeper sense of mystery, (an) "unknowableness of God"[10] that didn't exist prior.

Spiritual awareness versus formal religion

According to a 2003 Gallup poll, a significant percentage of the U.S. population claims to be spiritual but not religious.[11] What is the difference? Bush says that "religion is the organized, formal institution and spirituality [is the] private, inner connection with the Divine."[12]

Robert C. Fuller, a historian and professor of religious studies at Bradley University, writes:

> *Spirituality exists wherever we struggle with the issues of how our lives fit into the greater scheme of things. We encounter spiritual issues every time we wonder where the universe comes from, why we are here, or what happens when we die. We [are being] spiritual when we become moved by values such as beauty, love, or creativity that seem to reveal a meaning or power beyond our visible world...and [when we] desire to establish a felt-relationship with the deepest meanings or powers governing life.*[13]

Religion and resiliency

Many assume that those without religious faith have a harder time rebuilding their lives after the death of their partner than those who don't. Even though studies[14] generally confirm that organized religion is beneficial for emotional and physical health, one study[15] of resilience after spousal loss provided an unexpected result: those with *less* religious support often had greater possibilities for future growth than those who had significant religious support. It was concluded that those who had no formal beliefs possibly struggled more immediately after their loss and "the very struggle with its heightened stress may have generated stress-related growth."[16] This outcome reminds us to be cautious about making across-the-board assumptions about the role of religion and spirituality in others' lives.

TR·*ACTION*

I often use the following meditation with my clients to help them connect to an underlying energy that can orient and support them. Read the following several times until you are able to recite the meditation without having to stop and refer to this passage.

Sit in a comfortable chair with your back straight, feet on the ground, and hands on your knees or folded in your lap. Be sure the room temperature is not too cool.

Connect to your breathing. You might want to repeat silently "breathing in" as you inhale and "breathing out" as you exhale. Notice the air coming into your nostrils and then leaving. As you focus on your breathing, allow your breath to commence and end with your belly. You might think "soft belly" and say to yourself "belly rising" as you inhale and "belly falling" as you exhale.

As your breathing slows and steadies, repeat the following three statements — leaving several minutes of silence between each statement.

- "I am more than my body." (Long pause)
- "I am more than my mind." (Long pause)
- "I am more than my emotions" (Long pause as you sit with "what remains")

It will take four or five rounds of this meditation before you can do it without thinking about "what to do next." *Take the time.*

As your need to think takes a backseat to your experience, what remains?

Many people believe that what remains is what they brought into this world *before* they became aware of their body, mind, and emotions — an underlying consciousness and spiritual center that never changes.

> *Hal's reflections on life after the death*
> *of his wife from leukemia:*
> The worst part was having to deal with my guilt and the loneliness. I didn't think it would ever go away. It took six months before I was able to raise my head and see what was around me. Even now I miss her, and regret that our life focused on my own selfish behavior. I wish I had spent more time considering her happiness. It took years before I was willing to take responsibility for my responses. Thankfully, my life stabilized and I am a better person.
>
> If it hadn't been for Carmen's death, I wouldn't have changed my attitude toward my own mortality, met my current spouse, become closer with one of my two sons, and had counseling. I've also come to like being alone and even enjoy being a bit reclusive.

Notes

1. Kirkpatrick, Lee (1998). God as a substitute attachment figure: A longitudinal study of adult attachment style and religious change in college students. *Pers Soc Psychol Bull, vol. 24:9: pp 961–973.* doi: 10.1177/0146167298249004
2. Bush, Ashley Davis (1997). *Transcending Loss.* New York: Berkeley Press. p. 233.
3. Rosenblatt, Roger (2010). *Making Toast.* New York: Ecco.
4. Rosenblatt, Roger (2012). *Kayak Morning: Reflections on Love, Grief, and Small Boats.* New York: Ecco.
5. Wolpe, David (2009). *Why Faith Matters.* San Francisco: HarperOne.
6. *Ibid.* p. 136.
7. *Ibid.* p. 122.
8. Doka, Kenneth. (2002). How could God?: Loss and the spiritual assumptive world. In J. Kauffman (Ed.). *Loss of the assumptive world: A theory of traumatic loss.* (pp. 49–54). New York: Brunner-Routledge/

Taylor & Francis.

9. Lewis, C. S. (1961). *A Grief Observed*. New York, Bantam Books. pp. 9–10.

10. Doka, Kenneth. (2002). How could God?: Loss and the spiritual assumptive world. In J. Kauffman (Ed.). *Loss of the assumptive world: A theory of traumatic loss*. (pp. 49–54). New York: Brunner-Routledge/ Taylor & Francis.

11. Gallup, G., Jr. (2003). Americans' Spiritual Searches Turn Inward. Retrieved from http://www.gallup.com/poll/7759/americans-spiritual-searches-turn-inward.aspx.

12. Bush, Ashley Davis (1997). *Transcending Loss*. New York: Berkeley Press. p. 210.

13. Fuller, R. C. (2001). *Spiritual but Not Religious*. New York: Oxford University Press. pp. 8–9.

14. Chatters, L. (2000). Religion and health: Public health research and practice. *Annual Review of Public Health*, Vol. 21: 335-367. doi: 0.1146/annurev.publhealth.21.1.335.

15. Kelley, M. M., and Chan, K. T. (2012). Assessing the role of attachment to God, meaning and religious coping as mediators in the grief experience. *Death Studies*, 36:3, pp. 199–227.

16. *Ibid.* p. 222.

CHAPTER SIX

No Better Kickstart Than Being Petrified

Our real unconscious and underlying wish is to find a cure
for the impermanence of life and for that there is no remedy.
— David Whyte, *The Heart Aroused*

BEFORE THE death of your partner, your experience with death might have been limited to the elderly and/or "something that happened to other people." I'm not implying you didn't know *intellectually* that you would eventually die, but not knowing the date and not having suffered the loss of your mate helped you keep the monster under the bed.

And then everything changed.

Death came "up close and personal," as the saying goes, and the experience has likely brought with it a keen sense of your own fragile mortality: "If he/she can die, so can I." Like most individuals who have been close to the dying process, you have likely become less anxious about the actual act of dying and more introspective about your health, and the possibility of dying alone. In a nutshell, you might have chased the death monster from under your bed, but now you have to listen to wild dogs barking in your cellar.

Novelist Milan Kundera[1] writes that what terrifies us most about our death is not the loss of our future but the loss of our past, for it is our past that provides the evidence that we have lived. The Greek philosopher Epicurus contends that it is not the end of life that we fear; rather we fear that the end *is not* the end, in which case our anxiety is more focused on what we should have done in life and did not do.

Accepting your anxiety about death

Irwin Yalom, a Stanford psychiatrist and author of *Staring at the Sun: Overcoming the Terror of Death*[2], recounts how his clients' problems often stem from their feeling that they haven't really lived. Yalom has found over the years that the more his clients looked their mortality in the eye, the more liberated they were from the fear of it — *and* the more likely they were to use their anxiety as a catalyst for bringing more meaning, pleasure, and contentment in their lives.

Yalom suggests his clients regularly take a few minutes to relive *their current life over and over again for eternity*. Each time, it must remain exactly the same. No exceptions.

Take a minute, now, and imagine repeating the way you are choosing to live, over and over into eternity. Does the thought influence how you will begin tomorrow?

Denying one's death by procrastinating

Many people put things off because if they always have a lot to do, a part of them thinks they *can't* die. I wonder, are you a person who is always *needing to do but never doing?* When you think about procrastinating without pause into eternity — does taking action become appealing?

Taking it a step further, if you have money but don't know how to manage it, would it make sense to learn how or, alternatively, to hire a professional to do it for you? If your estate planning paperwork is a mess, could you arrange to get it cleared up? If you are physically out of shape, could you decide to do what is physically possible to get into better shape? If you feel unsafe, could you figure out what you need to do to feel safer? What would be the result of taking back your power and arranging for action? Think about it.

TR·*ACTION*

I've participated in hundreds of hours of training over the years, and I want to share an experiential exercise that I personally found valuable (although it turned out to be embarrassing and hysterically funny before it was over).

On the last day of a training, 15 of us were taken to a very large cemetery and told to walk for a minimum of 10 minutes in different directions. When we located a grave that seemed intriguing, we were instructed to lie down on the grave and remain motionless with our eyes open for 20 minutes. (Note: The management of the cemetery had approved our activity.)

I found a large family plot and proceeded to lie down and look up from the grave of a person who had died in the early 1900s. While thinking about my life having ended, I heard the sound of rustling fall leaves. Because I had seen squirrels tearing through the leaves earlier, I thought nothing of it until I looked up into the faces of five people standing in a circle over me.

Suddenly, I realized what was happening and bolted upright, awkwardly attempting to explain why I was lying on their family grave. None of the five people spoke a word in reply. As I walked back to the van, I could only imagine the story they'd tell about their cemetery visit.

Story told and humor aside, I invite you to take a blanket, find a quiet park or open space, and spend 20 minutes doing the same.

Afterward, jot down your answers to the following questions:

- What was the most frightening aspect of not being alive?
- Did the experience of "being dead" bring a new perspective to being alive?

TR·*ACTION*

This exercise is an extension of the previous one and is designed to help you accept both the uncertainty of the future and the fact that all things come to an end. Typically, the exercise is based on the concept of "dying into each day," but I am adapting it to "dying into each week."

Take a few minutes every Sunday night to imagine your life having ended. Stay with the feeling as long as it is tolerable. It may sound macabre, but it isn't. In practicing having died, you are more likely to 1) view your life as precious, 2) accept your fragility, and 3) remain strong in times of struggle.

The theme of this exercise parallels the Thai master's lesson about his drinking glass:

"You see this goblet?" asks Achaan Chaa, the Thai meditation master. "For me this glass is already broken. I enjoy it; I drink out of it. It holds my water admirably, sometimes even reflecting the sun in beautiful patterns. If I should tap it, it has a lovely ring to it. But when I put this glass on the shelf and the wind knocks it over or my elbow brushes it off the table and it falls to the ground and shatters, I say, 'Of course.' When I understand that the glass is already broken, every moment with it is precious."
— from Mark Epstein, *Thoughts Without a Thinker*[3]

When the master considers the goblet as already broken, he can open his mind to appreciate the time he has with the goblet. And if it breaks, he understands how fortunate he has been to have experienced the goblet.

Possibly you will begin to feel the same about your life — with practice.

End-of-Life Planning Resources

Wants, Wishes, and Wills: A Medical and Legal Guide to Protecting Yourself and Your Family in Sickness and in Health. By Wynne A. Whitman and Shawn D. Glisson. Financial Times Press, 2007.

Will and Trust Kit, by Suze Orman
(www.suzeorman.com)

Online Help (best to use an attorney)
Law Depot: www.lawdepot.com
Find Legal Forms: www.findlegalforms.com
Legal Zoom: www.legalzoom.com

Who Gets Grandma's Yellow Pie Plate? Workbook
University of Minnesota Extension
Service Distribution Center
20 Coffey Hall, 1420 Eckles Ave.
St. Paul, MN 55108-6068 • 800.876.8636

> **Sam's reflections on life after the death of his wife from breast cancer:**
>
> June's death changed my attitude about how to leave my own inheritance to my loved ones. The most difficult part of her death was my stepchildren trying to evict me from my home of 28 years. Thankfully, my lawyers negotiated a compromise.
>
> I first met the person who became my wife while we were involved in national charity organizational meetings. We saw each other professionally for two years, began dating, and married this year. I am happy. Looking back, I can see that I have grown as a man, and am now comfortable with my own death.

Notes

1. Kundera, Milan (1999). *Immortality.* New York: Harper Perennial Modern Classics.
2. Yalom, Irwin (2009). *Staring at the Sun: Overcoming the Terror of Death.* San Francisco: Jossey-Bass.
3. Epstein, Mark (2004). *Thoughts without a Thinker.* www.sbpoet.com.

CHAPTER SEVEN

The Surprising Truth about Negative Chatter

We don't see things as they are; we see things as we are.
— Anais Nin

Perceptions of widowhood

IN 2005, I asked a group of young widows and widowers — all
with teenagers at home — to shout out what came to mind
when they heard the word, "widow" or "widower." They were
stunned when they saw their final compiled list, a perfect example
of how easily we fall back on stereotypical thought patterns. Take
a look at what these middle-aged people had to say.

LABEL	RESULTING BEHAVIOR
OLD	Don't exercise
	Don't try anything new
	Stop paying attention to appearance
	Generally lose interest in oneself
ALONE	Isolated
	Don't volunteer
	Don't organize activity with others
	Wait to be called
	Refuse invitations
	Find an excuse not to participate
	Allow grief to define the rest of one's life

PITIFUL	Commit to live as if one's life is over
EMPTY	Don't seek activities that would be fullfilling
LOST	Don't make an effort; refuse to seek new territory
HELPLESS	Forget that the other side of the coin is "helpful"
SAD	Convince oneself that sadness is permanent
AFRAID/ANXIOUS	Don't take risks
ANGRY	Have a short fuse
JEALOUS	Resent those who are happy
CHEATED	Feel singled out: "Why me?"

While every stereotype starts with someone's historical truth, isn't it interesting how another era's negative belief can influence your self-perception — without being questioned?

Is it possible that you have stereotyped yourself in other ways as well?

Your belief system was complete by age six

No matter what your ethnic, religious, political, or national culture, the patterns and themes that make up your bedrock core beliefs were absorbed from family members' facial expressions, innuendo, actions, and spoken words. And they were securely in place by the time you were six years old.[1] Add in a dash of childhood peer experience, and you are set for life — unless you deliberately expose yourself to what is new, different, and uncomfortable long enough to broaden your view about yourself and the world in general.

For example, if your family followed the Methodist church while you were growing up, odds are that you have remained

60

a Protestant if you continue a religious practice — and you believe that it is a *preferred* religion. If your family was politically conservative, you also are likely to have a conservative mindset — and believe it to be the *right* mindset.

Going deeper, if you grew up with little money, you likely remain anxious about money, even if you are financially secure, because your belief system has not grown up. As a result, you perceive yourself to be a poor person with money rather than a person of wealth.

Moving to relationships, if you were led to believe that what you want is not important, you will accept chaotic, emotionally dysfunctional people into your life to prove you can't have what you want — a good relationship. In the same vein, if you were rejected as a child, you may desire acceptance as an adult and yet unconsciously create an environment in which you end up being rejected.

You might say you searched high and low for evidence to disprove your point of view, but "high and low" usually amounts to a hasty search through the lens of your preconceived beliefs that continue to limit rather than inform you. To further validate your perspective, you befriend people who have similar beliefs. Inevitably, what happens? *Credible information is dropped.*

While this may strike you as totally illogical, *a belief does not have to be logical or true.* If you subconsciously block data that could correct your erroneous core belief, what are you depending upon as fact? Your *perception* and *interpretation*.

Limiting beliefs are really small "t" truths

Your *interpretations* of the negative comments you received from family and friends while growing up are small "t" truths. Among the most common are: *I am not smart enough, tough enough, nice enough, tall enough, short enough, big enough, pretty enough, thin enough, handsome enough, or rich enough to do, be, or become what I would like.*

Another self-limiting small "t" truth might be that you are *worth-less* because you concluded long ago that you weren't as *worth-while* as one of your siblings. The bottom line: you may not share your self-limiting head chatter with others, but I doubt that you discount the self-talk as a false rumor.

Feeling alone? You aren't.

Everyone has had less-than-ideal childhood experiences, so no one escapes taking on some small "t" truths about his- or herself. However, with a little exploration, you may find that your childhood negative conclusions have little basis.

Take a safari into your deepest beliefs

Okay, let's do some speed-writing. Grab a pen or pencil, and answer the following prompts *without a moment of reflection*. Write as fast as you can without thinking. That's right! *Don't think* and *don't stop* until you have completed all of these sentences.

I will never be able to _____.

No one will ever _____.

Every time I start to _____I _____.

People think I am _____because

_____.

People don't know that I am_____.

The reason I don't have _____ is because

_____.

If only I could _____.

I can't _____ because I am not _____ enough.

If I did _____, people would find out that I

_____.

I will never get what I want because _____.

I won't ever be _____ because I am

_____.

No one will ever _____because I am

_____.

I don't deserve to _____because

_____.

When I am with friends, I feel I need to

_____.

As a kid I always felt_____.

People don't know that I _____.

Life is _____.

Marriage is_____.

Most women are _____.

Most men are _____.

You can't trust _____.

After completing the questions, review and reflect on your answers using the following list as a guide:

- Can you remember where and when you first became aware of the *rightness* of each belief?

- Are you sure you came to this belief on your own, or do you remember a parent living this belief?

- Has the belief helped you or hurt you while living your life?

- How is it affecting you now that you are faced with developing a new life path?

Beware of the influence of others

After the loss of your partner, you are not only at risk for being sabotaged by your own self-limiting beliefs, you are also vulnerable to being overly influenced by what others believe you should now be doing with your life. Peer and family pressure at any age can be powerful.

Author Jim Clemmer describes research on influence using

rhesus monkeys.[2] In one experiment, several rhesus monkeys are put into a specially designed room, and once a day a bunch of bananas are lowered through a hole in the ceiling. When the monkeys grab for a banana, they are hit with a blast of cold air causing them to drop the banana and move away. After a few days, the monkeys do not go near the bananas, even when the cold air is turned off.

Here is where the study becomes fascinating. Each day, one monkey is removed from the room and replaced with a new monkey — one that knows nothing of the cold blast of air. It is not surprising that the original monkeys still avoid the bananas. What *is* surprising is that a monkey new to the room also avoids the bananas! Interesting how easily they are influenced by others, isn't it?

Remember, you can't custom-build anything based on herd mentality. Stop and consider where you derive your locus of control — is it internal or external? Remember, it is *your* life so decisions that affect your life should be *yours*, don't you think?

As you read this chapter, you may be thinking this belief stuff is a real stretch: "I act the way I act because of my genes!" or "If it *is* true, what's done is done!"

Let's examine these reasons for not being the leader of your life.

"*I can't help it; it's genetic:*" If you believe that the way you perceive self, others, and events is primarily genetic, evidence-based research does not agree with you. While some of your traits and responses are innate, the majority of your personality is shaped by your experience and learning from infancy forward.[3]

"*What's done is done:*" Research confirms that people fall into two groups regarding how they view themselves. One group believes traits and beliefs are fixed (can't be changed), and the other thinks their beliefs are malleable (what we believe and how we function can be changed with effort and education).[4] Those in the malleable group find they can, indeed, change[5] because their brains get stronger with behavioral exercise and new connections are created as their brains learn new ways of believing[6]. Good news, don't you think?

We will spend more time later in the book on how you can overcome some of your self-limiting beliefs, but for now, I invite you to do the following experiential exercise to better understand the foundation of just one of your limiting beliefs.

TR·*ACTION*

Pick a "not enough" belief that you have carried since childhood. Go back to the first time you were aware of not feeling "enough."

What were the circumstances? _____

_____

How old were you? _____

Who was involved? _____

_____

Because you were using a child's ability to reason, could you have misinterpreted someone's intent or the circumstance?

_____

If not, what qualified the person/people to say or do what they did?

_____

Now close your eyes and enter the experience again. What did you learn about yourself and/or life from that experience?

_____

_____

Was your conclusion the only conclusion to be made? If, as an adult, you were now to witness a child in a similar circumstance, would your adult reasoning come to the same conclusion?

> *Margaret's reflections on life after the death of her husband from cancer:*
>
> After my husband's death, I didn't think I had what it would take to make clear, grounded decisions, confidently. It took three years before I felt emotionally healthy again. What helped most was being around others who had lost their spouses.
>
> During the second-year group, I was asked questions that I never would have thought I could answer, but I did. The class kicked me out and into the world to live again. I'm currently in a good relationship that's growing stronger. What I have in my new partner is what I wanted: someone who'd be different than my late husband, better even, and I have it. Also, my attitude toward how much I need to plan has changed. Now I concentrate on making the best decision for me in the moment.

Notes

1. Landers, Casey (2010). Early childhood development. Unicef House. http://home1.gte.net/pulsar/Library _Ref/Biology/ECD/ECD%20%20 2-6yrs.html.
2. Clemmer, Jim (2003). *The Leader's Digest: Timeless Principles for Team and Organization Success.* Toronto: Ecw Press.
3. Dwelk, C. (2008). Can Personality Be Changed? The role of beliefs in personality and change. *Association for Psychological Science, 17:6;* Roberts, B. W., Walton, K. E., and Viechtbauer, W. (2006). Patterns of mean-level change in personality traits across the life course: A meta-analysis of longitudinal studies. *Psychological Bulletin.* 132, 1–25.
4. Dwelk, C. (1999). *Self-theories: Their role in motivation, personality and development.* Philadelphia: Taylor and Francis/Psychology Press.
5. Aronson, J., Fried, C., and Good, C. (2002). Reducing the effects of stereotype threat on African American college students by shaping theories of intelligence. *Journal of Experimental Social Psychology*, 38, pp. 113–125.
6. Blackwell, I., Trzeniewski, K., and Dweck, C. (2007). Implicit theories of intelligence predict achievement across an adolescent transition: A longitudinal study and an intervention. *Child Development 78,* pp. 246–263.

CHAPTER EIGHT

Guess What Else Is Running the Show?

What we can't express runs our lives.
— Anonymous

W HAT IS going on when you make a new commitment and then back off, drag your feet, or stall rather than follow through?

Most people answer, "I don't know... over time, I guess it seemed less appealing" or "I decided I didn't have the energy" or "It was a pipe dream all along" or "The time came and went, and then it was too late" or "It sounded fun, but then I got busy doing something else and forgot about it."

I am sure you can come up with a few more, but most answers point to indecision created by a stronger, often unconscious, competing, and conflicting commitment.[1]

Usually the competing commitment is based on not wanting to feel fear or failure. Many of us live our lives not knowing why we only come close to grabbing what we want — before we blame others and circumstances for not getting it.

The following are variations of competing commitments:

- "I am more committed to feeling safe than getting what I want."

- "I am more committed to not failing than taking a risk."

- "I am more committed to not looking stupid than learning something new."
- "I am more committed to not being rejected than meeting new people."
- "I am more committed to not physically failing than entering into a relationship that might be sexually satisfying."
- "I am more committed to feeling safe than I am to traveling to unfamiliar places and having an amazing experience."

Subconscious commitments are NOT weaknesses

Competing commitments represent self-protection; they are natural and reasonable impulses. Yet most of us do not consciously realize the priority we place on protecting ourselves over and above seeking and accepting opportunities that will ultimately bring us pleasure.

Remember that the source of your fear and discomfort is *a thought*, not reality: you *have* thoughts but you are *not* your thoughts. Granted, you are entitled to have thoughts of discomfort, especially since you haven't been on your own in years. But can you *allow the discomfort you feel to just be* long enough to see it if it causes you to push away people and opportunities?

Observe yourself and others with curiosity

So how do you go about catching yourself during an interaction with another before an opportunity is totally out of sight? There are three elements to the secret sauce of social awareness: first, you observe yourself from your own point of view; second, you step into the other person's point of view during the ongoing exchange; and finally, you step back to gain some distance and observe both you and the other's comments and body language from a dispassionate perspective.[2]

What I just said sounds like a riddle, but read on to understand it better. It's a tool worth learning, if only to help you assess your own behavior in relation to others.

The *first perceptual position* is when you observe what is taking place through your own eyes as you see it (sympathy). When you interact with another, how do you use your body, your facial expression, and your language? Are you encouraging the other person to interact with you, or are you subtly pushing the other person away with your words and body language? Observe with curiosity any rising discomfort and resistance within your body. Explore the feeling and ask yourself what is driving your need to resist another's effort to connect to you.

Examples:

- "I'm not good enough to be this person's friend."

- "I can't do what they suggest because I've never done it before."

- "I'm going to refuse their invitation to _____ because I might make a fool of myself."

The *second perceptual position* is when you put yourself in another person's position (empathy), and you observe the inter-action from their perspective. How does the other person pre-sent his- or herself? Are they open and engaged, or closed? What could cause the other person to respond in this way? Can you understand their point of view? Could they be coming from their own fear — or are they reacting to the physical and verbal messages you are sending?

The *third perceptual position* is the position of the independent observer. You are in third position when you step back and observe yourself and the other person from a distance. It is a place of being *curious but detached,* much like watching two people interact in a movie. Because you are able to observe the entire scene, your thoughts and feelings might change dramatically as you better understand that what one of you does in this moment likely determines what the other person will do in the next.

If you think this moving from one position to another while engaging in short conversation is impossible, you'll be surprised to find that you can become quite good at it. And with your new awareness, you are more likely to feel a sense of compassion and acceptance for both yourself and the other person as you learn how body and verbal language can drive an interaction.

You can tolerate anything for the moment!

As you practice perceiving social interactions from different perceptual positions, notice how your mind and body soften when you remind yourself that 1) *you can tolerate anything for the moment* and 2) *what is taking place right now is okay.*

Tracy Goss says that life doesn't turn out as it should or as it shouldn't; rather it turns out as it does.[3] You already know that, don't you? But accepting that you are powerless to a certain degree can be empowering.

TR·*ACTION*

Being mindfully aware involves honest self-inquiry about how your thoughts and behavior affect your life. Read the following statements and use them to get in touch with your thoughts.

* *Right now I'm aware I'm lying to myself and everyone else about* _____

_____ .

* *Right now I'm aware that I feel threatened by people.*

* *Right now I'm aware that I don't like to admit when I am wrong.*

- *Right now I'm aware that being honest about my feelings scares me.*

- *Right now I'm aware that the reasons I give for doing and not doing something are a cover for what I don't want to admit.*

- *Right now I must be in control; if I am not, I* _____

_____ .

TR·*ACTION*

Odds are that you developed a childhood strategy to distance yourself from discomfort. Do any of the following labels describe your overall way of surviving life as a child?

The compliant one
The defiant one
The pleaser
The smart one
The funny one
The self-righteous intolerant one
The cute, flirty one
The born leader
The protector
The moderator/mediator
The tantrum-throwing hysteric
The caretaker (being present for others but not for yourself)
The entertainer
The victim
(Feel free to come up with your own)

How is your coping strategy working for you as an adult? While it is very difficult to stop leading, protecting, moderating, control-ling, or being funny, cute, smart, intolerant, emotional, or needy, relying on childhood strategies as an adult is like walking in the shoes you wore when you were 10 years old. They pinch!

After understanding the strategy you used to maintain comfort and control over your environment as a child, hold that childhood strategy in your left hand and your adult intention to rebuild your life in your right hand. Now close your eyes and bring the two together. Do they make a good team?

TR·*ACTION*

Roles vs. Roleless: If I had asked you to answer the question, "Who am I?" before your loved one's death, you would have likely answered by listing all of the roles that you filled within the relationship, in addition to the roles you held independent of your partner.

Now that you have survived the crisis of your loved one's death and lived alone for many months, your response may come from a deeper level as you ask, "Who, indeed, is this person I call me?" and "What do I need?" To help answer these questions, try the following exercise.

Imagine you are on a deserted island. The weather is mild, the wind calm, and the sea quiet and beautiful. You arrived without any roles, such as spouse, friend, companion, parent, son/daughter, friend, teacher, employee, employer, church member, athlete, volunteer, or caregiver.

As you sit isolated on the sand without any roles, how do you feel?

Write a brief description of who you are as a "roleless" person:

_____

_____

_____

Did you find it difficult to be a person without a role? Was the first answer that came to mind, "I am no one?" If so, that is not uncommon. To help you excavate who you are without your roles, think of yourself as one of those wonderful Russian nesting dolls that separates at the waist to expose another doll, which then opens to another and another, until you finally hold a doll that can't be divided. *It is from this forgotten undivided center that you can experience yourself honestly without pressure to be anyone other than who you are.*

In the coming months, live the question, *"who is this person I call me?"* Eventually your core — that place of strength and sensitivity that waits to be nurtured and appreciated — will make itself known.

Reminder: How are you coming with your Post-its®? Don't ignore this easy exercise. It will lead you to 1) what you know you will enjoy, 2) what you do not know much about but are open to trying, and 3) what is missing that is causing imbalance in your life.

> ***Susy's reflections on life after the death of her husband from cancer:***
>
> My husband was terminally ill for three years so I got used to thinking about life without him. Still the loss was enormous. I never expected to feel so alone, and I missed sharing with him.
>
> Looking back at the time of grief, it was like I was walking through a thick fog. I didn't start to feel emotionally healthy until I moved into my new home. Moving was pivotal to my healing.
>
> I love my new home, I've made new friends, and participate in lots of activities. I never expected to travel again, but I have been to Asia, Europe, and South America in the last seven years. I found that I am strong and can take care of myself quite well.

Notes

1. Kegan, Robert and Lahey, Lisa (2001). *How the Way We Talk Can Change the Way We Work*. San Francisco: Jossey-Bass/Wiley.
2. Andreas, Connie Rae (1994). *Core Transformation*. Boulder: Real People Press.
3. Goss, Tracy (1995). *The Last Word on Power*. New York: Crown Business.

CHAPTER NINE

Change Your Body Language, Change Your Life

The body says what words cannot.
— Martha Graham

THE PREVIOUS chapter discussed tracking the three perceptual positions as you interact with another person. Now it's time to go deeper and understand how your body posture and facial expressions affect your thoughts and influence the way you act.

In her manual, *Degriefing: The Art of Transforming Grief*, Lyn Prashant writes about recognizing the look of grief: "We seem to innately comprehend the immense pain of a grieving person by seeing their haggard expression, blank stare, rolled shoulders, slumped posture, and listless walk."[1]

With time, most of these physical characteristics correct themselves, but a few might have become learned habits. Take a moment, right now, to become aware of your posture. Are you standing or sitting with your chest open or closed? If it's closed, how is your mind interpreting the meaning of your physical posture? Several research studies will help you answer the question.

A 2009 study by Richard Petty, Ohio State University professor of psychology, found that our posture affects not only how others think of us but also how we think of ourselves. Writes Petty:

> *Most of us were taught that sitting up straight gives a good impression to other people, but it turns out that our posture can affect how we think about ourselves. If you sit up straight, you end up convincing yourself by the posture you're in. People assume their confidence is coming from their own thoughts. They don't realize that their posture is affecting how much they believe in what they are thinking.*[2]

Petty found similar results when it came to head nodding. People had more confidence in the thoughts they generated when they nodded their heads up and down compared to when they shook their heads from side to side.

In a third study published in the January 2011 issue of *Psychological Science,* researchers tested open and constricted postures. They found that when individuals open their bodies and occupy space, a sense of power is activated in the mind that allows them to feel and behave as if they are in charge.[3]

It's particularly interesting that the sense of power produced by posture expansiveness did not depend on the person's title or position of power. For example, the person without a title felt more confident when physically open than the person with a high-powered position whose body was in a constricted position.

Shifting from a psychological perspective to a physiological one, Carney and Cuddy of Harvard Business School had 26 females and 16 males participate in a study[4] in which half of the participants held two expansive postures for one minute each and the other half held two lower-power postures for one minute each. When tested for neuroendocrine hormone levels, the high-power posers showed higher levels of testosterone (closely linked to an ability to adapt) and lower levels of cortisol (a stress hormone).

Using the body to manage the mind

A joint study by researchers from the University of Singapore and the University of Chicago asked a group of volunteers to 1) immerse their hands in ice water, 2) drink water and vinegar, or 3) watch a video of injured children after the Haiti earthquake. Half the group was told to clench a muscle in their body as they took part in the experiments, while the other half wasn't given any instructions about what to do. Those who tightened a muscle during the experience reacted more positively at every point. The study states:

> *Participants who were instructed to tighten their muscles, regardless of which muscles they tightened — hand, finger, calf, or biceps — while trying to exert self-control, demonstrated greater ability to withstand the pain, consume the unpleasant medicine, attend to the disturbing but essential information, or overcome tempting foods, showing the mind and the body are so closely tied together, merely clenching muscles can also activate willpower.*[5]

Now you have no excuses. With this information and a little practice, you can add an important ally — your body — to your toolbox for rebuilding your life.

Touch tells your mind and body that you are safe

Leonard Mlodinow, author of *How Your Unconscious Mind Rules Your Behavior*,[6] reports that when you say your feelings are hurt, you are correct. "Hurt feeling" means pain: a combination of unpleasant emotional feelings and a feeling of sensory distress. Anyone who has grieved the loss of a loved one knows that grief hurts all over. Not surprisingly, a University of Michigan study showed that emotional pain activates the same region of the brain as physical pain.[7]

In the film, *Touch: The Forgotten Sense*[8], researchers filmed a library checkout desk. After checking out a book, each person was asked to rate his or her experience. Those who had accidentally brushed the librarian's hand reported a more enjoyable experience than those who had not made contact. Even more surprising, people did not have to be aware of being touched to say they had a better experience than the control group (those who had not been touched).

The same held true for those eating in a restaurant. If the waiter touched a diner, the diner reported a more enjoyable experience and left a larger tip, compared to those who had no physical contact.

Cuddling and cholesterol

Scientists at Ohio State University published a study wherein rabbits were fed diets high in cholesterol. Oddly, one group of rabbits did not test high in cholesterol. Further investigation determined that the technician cuddled the unaffected group of rabbits when feeding them. As a result, different neuropeptides transmuted the cholesterol into a completely different metabolic pathway eliminating the rise in cholesterol.[9]

TR·*ACTION*

Clearly, touching and being touched has advantages. If you are not in the habit of being casually physical, consider changing your behavior to maintain your health. For example, schedule a manicure, pedicure, or massage. To economize, contact your local junior college and ask if it offers a massage certification program. If so, you can book a massage at a low price. The program depends on people in the community making appointments with those in training.

At the very least, touch another's wrist or forearm during a conversation. Why? Because *you cannot touch another without being touched yourself.*

TR·*ACTION*

Sit in a chair and roll your shoulders forward and drop your head. Notice how you feel emotionally. Next slowly unroll and expand your chest, then lift your head and then lift your chin slightly. Do you feel emotionally stronger?

Maintaining this expanded position, close your eyes and smile. How does your smile affect the emotional tone of your body-mind? Interesting, eh?

What your brain communicates to your body depends on the message your body first sent to your brain. In effect, there is a feedback loop: when you are happy you smile, when you smile, you feel happier. In other words, your brain and body are in a constant conversation, each able to affect the other.[10]

Marti's reflections on life after her husband died of a heart attack:

At the time of Brad's death, I didn't think I was capable of raising my kids alone. It was a terrible struggle, and I didn't start to feel emotionally healthy for two years.

I resented my friends comparing death with divorce, or saying I would remarry because I was young. Happily, I have rebuilt my life and I did fall in love again. My faith in Jesus Christ has helped. It's Christ I held onto when my world imploded.

If it hadn't been for Brad's death, I never would have known that I could be a good single parent, make a career change, and move to another part of the country.

Notes

1. Prashant, Lyn (2002). *Degriefing: The Art of Transforming Grief.*
2. Petty, Richard (2009). Body posture affects confidence in your own thoughts. Research done at Ohio State University and also appeared in the October 2009 issue of the *European Journal of Social Psychology.* http://researchnews.osu.edu/archive/posture.htm.
3. Huang, L. (2010). Powerful Postures Versus Powerful Roles: Which Is the Proximate Correlate of Thought and Behavior? *Psychological Science,* January 2011 22: pp. 95–102, first published on December 13, 2010. doi:10.1177/0956797610391912.
4. Carney, D. R., Cuddy, A. J. C., and Yap, A. J. (2010). Power posing: brief nonverbal displays affect neuroendocrine levels and risk tolerance. *Association of Psychological Science.* DOI:0.1177/0956797610383437.
5. Huang, I. W., and Labroo, A. A. (2011). From Firm Muscles to Firm Willpower: Understanding the Role of Embodied Cognition in Self-Regulation. *Journal of Consumer Research.* Vol. 37, No. 6 (April 2011), pp. 1046–1064. The University of Chicago Press. Article Stable http://www.jstor.org/stable/10.1086/657240.
6. Mlodinow, Leonard (2012). *Subliminal: How Your Unconscious Mind Rules Your Behavior.* New York: Pantheon.
7. Kross, E., Berman, M. G., Mischel, W., et al. (2011). Social rejection shares somatosensory representations with physical pain. *Proceedings of the National Academy of Sciences.* doi: 10.1073/pnas.1102693108.
8. *Touch: The Forgotten Sense* (2001). Film produced by Max Films. http://www.imdb.com/title/tt0903652/.
9. Chopra, D., and Simon, D. (2002). *Grow younger, live longer.* New York: Three Rivers Press.
10. Conner, Marcia (2004). *Learn More Now.* Hoboken, NJ: John Wiley & Sons.

CHAPTER TEN

Wired or Tired: Great Times to Act

Although every man believes that his decisions and resolutions
involve the most multifarious factors, in reality they
can be an oscillation between flight and longing.
— Herman Broch, Austrian writer

A s you move further away from the death of your partner
and become more comfortable with your independence,
you may experience waves of unexplained sadness. This
is understandable. Part of you is grieving for the person you
once were, while another part is adapting to the person you are
becoming. This period of time is often referred as the shift from
pre-loss to post-loss meaning.[1]

While you may be enjoying life more, making major decisions
without your partner's input can still cause panic. To control this
sense of panic, it is important to understand that every activity
and decision includes a sequence of actions that you've done
innumerable times.

Let's use the simple example of taking a shower. If you are
a guest in someone else's home or staying in a motel/hotel, you
must adapt your usual routine of 1) removing the clothes you are
wearing, 2) finding a place for your products and towel, and 3) de-
ciding where you are going to dress. But does the need to reorder
your usual sequence of actions stop you from washing your hair

and body, drying off, or dressing? Of course not.

This example carries a simple truth. Everything you do is made up of a combination of routine actions, such as walking, talking, eating, drinking, reading, using the phone, driving a car, meeting people, introducing yourself, listening, planning, and taking and following directions. True, the context may be new, or what you label the activity may cause it to *feel* new. But if you think about it, you've done everything required to start and complete that particular activity thousands of times.

Low- and high-stakes decisions

Once you understand that every activity is a matter of reordering a sequence of familiar actions, the next thing for you to grasp is how quickly you will discount what I have just said when it comes to high-stakes decisions.

After all, taking a shower is nothing compared to buying a car, taking a trip, or dating, right? True, the reason the stakes are higher is because there is a financial or emotional cost involved, which generally means *you might have to live with what you do not like*. And there's the kicker! The very thought of making a mistake can cause you to panic and feel unqualified to move forward.

But the only significant difference between low- and high-stakes decisions is that high-stakes decisions require more *thought*, possible *research*, and elementary *planning*. But you have thought, learned, and planned throughout your entire life, regardless of whether you have been in the workforce or in the home raising children. So…when it comes time to think about buying a new car, you may not have been in charge of previous car purchases, but you do know how to do it — well!

When is the best time to do what you intend to do?

There are decades of chronobiologic research[2] regarding both *circadian* (24-hour biological cycle) and *ultradian* rhythms (recurring cycles within the circadian cycle) and how they affect the outcome of medical procedures and the timing of medication. For our purposes, let's examine how to best use waking ultradian energy cycles to your advantage. During your waking hours, you cycle through daily 90- to 120-minute energy cycles, after which you lose focus.[3] While your natural inclination might be to power through the drop in energy, research shows that if you stop for 15 to 20 minutes and shift to another type of task, your overall productivity increases.[4]

If, for example, you are doing something physical and feel your energy drop, shift to a mental activity such as reading a book or magazine. On the other hand, if you find yourself distracted when involved in intense thinking, shift to something physical like a short walk.

In addition to the ultradian rhythm shifts, you are also better at certain types of activities at specific times of day. A recent *Wall Street Journal* article summarized when a person is most productive. (Note: the results are for the waking hours of an average person. If you are an extreme morning or night person, adjust the timing backward or forward.

- Work that requires concentration is best performed in the late morning. Why? Because one's body temperature starts and continues to rise through midday, and working memory improves as the temperature rises. Note: taking a warm shower after midday helps.[5]

- The ability to concentrate typically starts to slide midday, with most people distracted from noon until 4 p.m.[6]

- Alertness slumps after a meal, with drowsiness peaking around 2 p.m., making that a good time for a 15–45 minute nap (longer than that is counterproductive, by the way).[7]

- If you are a creative person, you will be heartened to learn that the *best time for creative thinking is when you are fatigued*. It is thought that fatigue might allow the mind to wander more freely, to explore alternative solutions. How nice that you can be creative when you are tired.[8]

TR·*ACTION*

The next time you consider participating in an activity that causes you to feel anxious, practice taking it apart, action by action, and then try to find a single behavior you haven't done many times before.

Is your mind currently racing to prove me wrong? Okay, I understand. Perhaps you have never cooked a meal in your life, but let's face it, if you can read, you can read a recipe; if you can walk, you can go to a grocery store and shop. And I know that you have used your hands many times to turn a knob so you can turn on the stove. And you have certainly held and used a knife before. And if you have ever washed your car, you can wash pots and pans.

Can't dance? I challenge you to break down what is considered dancing. If you can take a step to the right, left, forward, and back in random order, then you can dance. If you have held both of your arms up in the air, you can hold the hands of your dance partner as you dance. If you have smiled before, you can smile while dancing and convince yourself that you are enjoying yourself!

ONGOING TR·*ACTION*

Expanding your Post-it® notes

Now that you know that you are creative when you are drowsy, take advantage of times of fatigue to detail some of the two-word or three-word Post-it® notes you made.

Let's say you made a Post-it® note last week that reads "relationship." Instead of simply wanting to be in a relationship, consider buying a drugstore notebook and start to detail *what kind of relationship* you would like. While thinking clearly won't prevent another person from hiding bad behavior, detailing the type of relationship you want will lower the risk of later unhappiness.

The following examples show you how to expand on your initial thoughts. Don't make this a one-time activity. Keep your Post-it® notebook close by so you can easily add to your list of details.

Travel:

- I want to travel.
- I want to take a low-key trip to _____.
- I want to take an educational trip but I also want to have fun.
- I want to go to Italy, take a cooking class, and then explore the hill towns.
- I want to take an adventurous trip.
- I want to volunteer in another country.
- I want to go to _____ and rent a furnished apartment for a month.
- I want to travel only in the U.S.

Friends:

- I want new friends.
- I want new, interesting friends.
- I want new friends who are interested in what I'm interested in.
- I want new friends who like to travel.
- I want new friends who like to read.
- I want more friends who _____.
- I want fewer friends who _____.

Active Lifestyle:

- I want to be active.
- I want to be active in _____.
- I want to be active in _____ but I don't want it to take up all my time.
- I want to be active in _____ for six months to see if I like it.
- I want to be active in solo activities.
- I want to be active in group activities.
- I want to try many different activities and find out which ones I like.

One-on-One Relationship:

- I want to be in a relationship.
- I want to be in a good relationship.
- I want to be in a good permanent relationship.
- I want to be in a good permanent relationship with a loving,

generous, kind person.

- I want to be in a good permanent relationship with a loving, generous, kind person who likes my kids.

- I want to be in a good permanent relationship with a loving, generous, kind person who likes my kids, and whom my kids like as well.

- I want to be in a good relationship but not live with the person.

- I want to be in a good relationship with someone who likes to travel.

- I want to be in a good relationship with someone who doesn't want to travel.

If you develop a few detailed parameters without becoming obsessed with the process, you will not only be less anxious as you approach your future, but you will also be less impulsive. And yes, risk is involved — always. But to be fully alive, you must act in the face of risk and accept that your life is in a constant state of evolution.

One caveat: don't become so enamored with detail that you become blind to what you could very well enjoy but don't know about.

Trudy's reflections on life after her partner died of cancer:

The worst part was being alone, while getting reacquainted with myself. The biggest hurdle was not having Sue for a sounding board. I resented having to make all of the decisions alone.

In group, I watched everyone take baby steps, then bigger ones — and I did the same. Since then, I have changed my attitude toward death, and I have changed my mind about my own strength and compassion. One doesn't know one's strength until it is tested.

With Sue's death, I was forced to confront a lot of things about myself. Now I am in a very healthy relationship — happier than I ever thought possible.

Notes

1. Neimeyer, R.A., Holland, J.M., et al. (2008). Meaning reconstruction in later life: Toward a cognitive-constructivist approach to grief therapy. In: Gallagher-Thompson, D., Steffan, A., Thompson, L., editors. Handbook of behavioral and cognitive therapies with older adults, pp. 264–277. New York: Springer-Verlag; Wortman, C.B., and Boerner, K. (2007). In H.S. Friedman and R.C. Silver (Eds.), *Foundations of Healthy Psych.* pp. 285–324. New York: Oxford University Press; Bonanno, G. A., Wortman, C. B., and Nesse, R. M. (2004). Prospective patterns of resilience and maladjustment during widowhood. *Psychology and Aging*, 19(2), pp. 260–271.
2. Smolensky, M.H., and D'alonzo, G. E. (1993). Medical Chronobiology: Concepts and Applications. *Am. J. Respir. Crit. Care Med.*, 147:S2–S19.
3. Rossi, E. (1990). The eternal quest: Hidden rhythms of stress and healing in everyday life. *Psychological Perspectives*, 22, pp. 6–23.
4. Rossi, E. (1993). The psychobiology of mind-body healing. Rev Ed. New York: W. W. Norton; Rossi, E., and Lippincott, B. (1992). The wave nature of being: Ultradian rhythms and mind-body communication.

In Lloyd, D., and Rossi, E. (Eds.) *Ultradian Rhythms in Life Processes: An Inquiry into Fundamental Principles of Chronobiology and Psychobiology*. pp. 371–402. New York: Springer-Verlag.
5. Hirota, T., Wook, J., St. John, P., et al. (2012). Identification of small molecule activators of cryptochrome. *Science*, July 12 issue. doi: 10.1126/science.1223710.
6. Matchock, R., and Mordkoff, J.D. (2012). Chronotype and time-of-day influences on the alerting, orienting, and executive components of attention. *Research Gate* 192(2): pp. 189–198.
7. Moore-Ede, Martin (1994). *The Twenty-Four-Hour Society: Understanding Human Limits in a World That Never Stops*. Boston: Addison Wesley.
8. Wieth, M. B., and Zacks, R. T. (2011). Time-of-day effects on problem solving: When the non-optimal is optimal. *Thinking & Reasoning*, 17, pp. 387–401.

Eating Well

Set aside those "heart-healthy" frozen dinners and consider eating fresh food that doesn't carry a label. If your food does have a label, remember that having fewer ingredients translates into fewer additives such as sugar, salt, and preservatives.

Don't tell your physician you are eating well if you aren't. Why? Because if you aren't, the physician will likely say it is appropriate to take a quality daily vitamin and mineral supplement.

Exercise and Bodywork

Did you know that establishing a new habit takes about three weeks? Yes, exercise can become a habit like any other. Why not commit to 21 days of moderate exercise and then determine what you're going to do on the 22nd day? Consider one or two of the following:

- Walk for at least 15 to 30 minutes each day, if possible. If not, take a longer walk three times a week.
- Go to a nearby fitness center for a moderate workout. AARP Silver Slippers offers a senior discount at some of the large fitness centers.
- Consider taking a weekly therapeutic/restorative yoga or basic stretch class. In addition explore joining a tai chi or qigong class.
- Do you like to dance? If so, put on some music and dance at home for 15 minutes a day, even if you are able to move only the top half of your body while sitting in a chair.

I highly recommend the bestselling book, *Younger Next Year — Live Strong Until You're 80 and Beyond*, by Chris Crowley and Dr. Henry Lodge (Workman Publishing, 2007). It is a quick read for every age group, and it provides the best explanation of how aerobic exercise can physiologically turn back the decay of aging. The authors wrote the original book for both sexes, but they have recently published a women's edition entitled *Younger Next Year for Women*.

CHAPTER ELEVEN

Ditch Willpower for the Power of Pretend

We are what we repeatedly do.
— Aristotle

D ANIEL SIEGEL, physician and clinical professor of psychiatry at the UCLA School of Medicine, says, "Grief allows us to let go of something we've lost only when we begin to accept what we now have in its place."[1] In a general sense, I agree with what Siegel says, but I want to emphasize that "accepting what you now have" is not an end — in and of itself.

Gaining physical and emotional stability after the death of a life partner is an exhausting accomplishment — one that requires privacy so that you can express emotion, sleep when sleep comes, and move, read, and write when motivated. While such isolation is required to cope with the reality of the death, hopefully it is only the beginning of what you will accept in life.

As you move toward better days, your imagination will be key to unlocking your ability to accept significant change, comfortably. To develop a baseline sense of how you are currently imagining your future, close your eyes and "picture" your life without your companion. Okay, you just used your imagination!

Now let's learn how to make better use of what you imagine.

The power of your prefrontal cortex

Harvard psychologist Dan Gilbert recently gave a TED talk about how the brain evolved over a two-million-year period from a mere quarter of a pound to the three-pound mass you currently carry in your head. The added heft includes a new section called the frontal lobe of which the prefrontal cortex is the most important part. It is the prefrontal cortex that *allows you to experience something in your mind before you try it in real life.* Gilbert calls it your "experience simulator" because it functions in the same way a flight simulator functions for people who are learning to fly — by acting *as if* they are flying first.

Charles Garfield, who worked on the NASA simulator program for the astronauts, is now head of the Performance Institute in Berkeley, California, and studies performance in general. In his book, *Athletes,* Garfield tells of a visualization study conducted by Soviet scientists prior to the 1980 Olympics in Lake Placid, New York. The Soviets divided their outstanding athletes into four groups:

- Group 1: did 100% physical training.
- Group 2: did 75% physical training, 25% mental training.
- Group 3: did 50% physical training, 50% mental training.
- Group 4: did 25% physical training, 75% mental training.

The results showed that Group 4 had greater improvement than group 3; Group 3 more improvement than Group 2; and Group 2 more improvement than Group 1. Clearly the group that spent the most time imagining themselves doing well performed significantly better than those who dedicated their time only to physical training.[2] The point of citing these examples is not for you to perfect your physical performance but to understand the power of your mind.

From a neuroscientific point of view, each time you visualize yourself doing something, a neural pathway is created, that is, your body's circuitry is stimulated *as if* you are having a real-life experience. And with each subsequent similar visualization, you strengthen that connection in the same way you create a visible path by repeatedly walking upon the same area of grass.

Thankfully, fMRI* technology enables science to validate that the same area of your brain lights up whether you are eating a piece of chocolate cake or imagining that you are eating a piece of chocolate cake.[3]

You are always imagining something

Have you ever considered that "what you focus on you amplify?"[4] Michael Yapko, clinical psychologist, author, and expert on depression, emphasizes the importance of being aware of this phenomenon. When I asked you earlier to imagine your expected future, did you see yourself as full of life, confidently seeking new friends, interests and activities, or were the images quiet and void of feeling? Whatever the overall tone of your image, it will be mentally reinforced until you change your vision.

A young father once told me that his primary focus was to make sure that he worried — explaining that he used worry as a strategy to manage his fear of uncertainty and prevent bad things from happening. In an attempt to sound logical, he said he wasn't sure how it worked, but he believed that if he constantly *imagined* the worst happening, he could prevent what he *imagined* from happening. And in his defense, occasionally something that he worried about would happen, which unfortunately reinforced his argument for the need to *imagine* the worst.

---

* fMRI stands for a "functional" MRI, which measures how the brain is functioning as opposed to a traditional MRI, which measures structure and is used for the diagnosis of disease.

Yapko comments that when people get into this kind of tailspin, they are *failing to differentiate probability from possibility.* Yes, it was possible that something the young man worried about would happen, but was it probable? Was it a real concern or just noise?

To summarize, it is important to understand that if you focus on feelings of fear and anxiety, you are envisioning a negative reality *as if* it were happening *right now,* and if you focus on having courage and being curious, you are imagining a positive reality *as if* it were happening *right now.*

In either case, your subconscious mind accepts, without question, your current image as reality. And with each similar image and thought, your brain lays down another neural pathway to reinforce your previous pathways, amplifying what you have focused on.

Now, stop reading for a minute and ask yourself, "Am I imaging my weaknesses or strengths?" "Am I focused on what is going right or what is going wrong?" "Is what I'm amplifying likely to hinder or help me rebuild my life?"

How the conscious versus unconscious (non-conscious) work together

Your conscious mind, which analyzes, evaluates, and makes decisions, represents roughly five percent of the overall function of your mind. *The balance of your mental activity is determined by your non-conscious, or unconscious, mind, which allows you to move through your day automatically accomplishing what needs to be done.*[5] Specifically, your unconscious manages your body's cardiovascular, pulmonary, skeletal, digestive, and immune systems. It also stores all of your previous experience, forgotten memories, and the life strategies that you develop to keep yourself safe at all costs.

You might find it difficult to grasp that your conscious mind accounts for so little because 1) it is all you are aware of, and 2) it never seems to shut up so it hardly seems insignificant, right? To better understand, let's look at how both parts of your mind function when you drive a car.

When you first learned to drive, you made a conscious effort to remember the complex interplay of tasks involved. And, initially, your conscious mind found it difficult to simultaneously perform so many actions. But once your conscious mind learned how to drive, it turned the task over to your unconscious mind to automatically implement.

Now, when you choose to drive, all you need is your conscious intention and a car key to drive from point A to point B without recalling how to steer, brake, shift gears, or look into side or rearview mirrors — *unless* something unusual takes place on the highway. Then, your unconscious immediately alerts your conscious mind to come forward and analyze how to bypass the potential danger.

This process of consciously learning and then turning over what you learned to your unconscious has been going on since you were an infant. When you saw something you wanted, you imagined grabbing it and then physically crawled to complete the vision. When crawling became too slow, you envisioned yourself walking and then running — and then did both — cutting your time. Once you met your first street curb, you learned to pick up one foot and place it on top of the curb, and then followed with your other foot. The next time you came upon a curb, you didn't stop and wonder how to step up onto the curb because you could easily envision the completed task.

So if that is all true, why is it so hard to envision getting what you need — now? The most significant difference between then and now is that *then* you were eager to acquire one new experience after another. With the death of your life partner, you are given no choice. Also, because you were together for so long, it can seem like you *are* having to learn how to crawl, walk, run, and step up onto a curb all over again. However, it is important for you to acknowledge that the same imagination you used as an infant is still available for you to develop fresh eyes for your future.

How perception created a reality for Harvard volunteers

In 1985, Ellen Langer conducted a Harvard study[6] with elderly volunteers. They were isolated during a two-week retreat with all evidence of the current year removed. Langer then asked the volunteers to live *as if* they were living in 1959. Each was given clothing of that era and was invited to watch movies, listen to music, and read newspapers and magazines only from 1959.

At the end of the two-week period, the participants' vision, hearing, perception, strength, and even finger length were measured. *The majority were found to have regressed several years in age — in all measures.* Many months later, the researchers retested the same individuals, and all the indications of being physically younger had disappeared. Why?

Who they were was dependent on their *perception* of age.

Moving from the world of academia to small town America

Moving from the venerable halls of ivy, what did widow Grandma Moses focus on and amplify when, at age 78, she quit needlepointing and started to paint? You might assume that she had showed signs of early talent, but consider the following about the widow named Anna Mary Robertson:

- Starting at age 12, she cleaned the houses of the wealthy in Greenwich, New York, until she married Thomas Moses at age 27.
- Thomas managed a horse ranch, and Anna bought a cow,

churned butter, and made and sold potato chips.

- After her husband's death, Anna's daughter taught her to create a picture out of embroidery yarn. But soon, she wasn't able to hold a needle because of the arthritis in her hands. Her sister Celestia suggested she paint instead, and off she went on another adventure.

- The druggist's wife offered to put Moses's paintings in their small town drugstore window. One day, a New York collector named Louis Caldor came through town and bought every one of her paintings. Later, Caldor contacted Anna to tell her that he was going to take her paintings to the New York museums. Hearing that, the Moses family thought Caldor was nuts.

- In 1939, the Museum of Modern Art accepted three of Moses's paintings.

- Shortly after, Gimbels department store in New York City featured her art in its windows for a Thanksgiving festival and invited her to speak. She came to the city wearing a small black hat and a white lace-collared dress.

- Soon Grandma Moses signed a greeting card contract with Hallmark and later received a special award from President Harry Truman.

- In 1953, she appeared on the cover of Time magazine; in 1960, Life magazine did a feature article on her 100th birthday.

- She finished her 1,500th canvas at age 101.

I chose an elderly person as an example because if the elderly can focus and amplify the positive, those of us who are younger should have an easier time of developing this tool.

The difference between your imagination and your willpower

Most of us have been convinced of what is possible and appropriate by our ethnic, national, religious, medical, and family cultures. If we decide to change something that is within our perceived scope of possibility, we call upon our willpower rather than taking the easier route of using our imagination to make the change. And that is understandable. That is what we have been taught to do!

I'm sure you've heard of repeating positive affirmations daily in order to master change. Granted the process can be effective in the short term but, like a New Year's resolution, the change is usually short-lived. Why? Because willpower is a conscious action, it comes from force and is usually based upon self-restraint.

Remember, your conscious mind is the part that judges and analyzes. Therefore, as you repeat a positive affirmation over and over, your conscious mind quickly (but erroneously) assesses that *if* what you are repeating *were* possible, you would be living it instead of yapping about it over and over!

What your conscious mind CAN do

Your conscious mind can, however, help you analyze your self-limiting beliefs once they are exposed for what they are — which means you can stop living on automatic pilot.

Once you have more control, you *can* consciously shift your focus off of what you don't want and onto what you do. In doing this you reinforce your inner resources, imagination, and strengths, rather than your weaknesses. And yes, initially, there will be an emotional clash between wanting to step back and settle for what comes easily and wanting to step forward and tolerate the discomfort that comes with the new — but as your subconscious view of reality changes (your vision), your ability to respond differently increases.

Robert Fritz writes that you will never like a limiting belief that tends to hang around, but by using your unconscious mind to *affect the way you view the belief,* your not-enough thought can transform into a more functional version, such as "boy, for a guy who is stupid, I am doing pretty well."[7]

When you repress positive images, you repress a positive future

In conclusion, the tool for accessing your unconscious mind is your imagination. If you wish to add vitality to your years, practice using your senses to imagine (rehearse) desirable circumstances *as if they're happening right now* — in spite of your reservations.

As you repeatedly experience *believed-in imaginings,* your conscious mind will stop analyzing and your non-conscious mind will accept that you are able to do what is necessary — quite comfortably. Remember the brain doesn't know the difference between the real and the imagined.

Before we move into exercises, you may be thinking, "This won't work because I can't see anything when I close my eyes." My response: "Really?"

When clients say they can't visualize, I ask them which wall their bed is against and how many nightstands they have. They can always give me the details. Then I ask them the color of car they drive, and they can tell me that as well. Soon, they realize that when I ask the question, an image flashes through their mind. While it is true that some of us can visualize images more vividly than others, images normally flash through our minds on a steady basis.

Dan Gilbert used an outrageously comical example in his TED talk to prove that your prefrontal cortex can imagine quite well: *Why didn't Ben and Jerry's ever develop a liver-and-onion ice cream?* Well, how about that? You quickly and successfully imagined how awful that would taste! So remember, your imagination isn't just limited to what you are able to see and picture.

How the class members perceived Betsy's trip

Betsy recently came to class after missing two sessions. She had called to say that she "had a conflict" so I mailed her the handouts so she could stay current. "Learning sideways" happened to be the topic for the evening she returned.

As members of the group started to talk, Betsy piped up and said, "Well, without knowing what it is, I have been learning sideways for eight weeks!" Everyone listened in awe as Betsy described how she and her cousin took her cousin's car with a full tank of gas, little luggage, no particular destination, and not a single reservation — and drove for two months across the United States and back. They had two rules for their trip: 1) they would stop when something looked interesting, and 2) they would change directions any time it occurred to them.

As she finished speaking, group members responded in amazement: "I can't *see* myself doing that! (visual)." "That doesn't *sound* like something I could do (auditory)." "That kind of trip wouldn't be a *good fit* (kinesthetic) for me. It doesn't *feel* right (kinesthetic) to just leave without plans." Everyone was using their imagination but not necessarily in the same way.

While we all use our five senses on a regular basis, usually one sense predominates with a second not far behind. For example, a person can be primarily visual but also have a strong auditory sense.

If you watch television or read magazines, you have had the experience of subconsciously identifying with being healthy and happy when viewing advertisements. A similar experience takes place when you enter a house that is for sale. How do you assess a house that is empty versus a house that is staged with furniture, art, towels in the bathrooms, and lawn furniture outside? What is the difference? When a home is full of furniture and there is soap and towels in the bathrooms, don't you automatically *see* and *feel* yourself living in the home? Of course you do. By using your imagination, you are able to bypass the discomfort that comes with the unfamiliar.

TR·*ACTION*

Expand your environment

Close your eyes and think of yourself as a goldfish. Get a sense of what it feels like to be in a small bowl in which you have little room to grow. Then shift your focus to how it feels to be outside in a protected, in-the-ground pond where your ability to move around and grow is unlimited.

Why did I ask you to imagine being a goldfish? Because how you live is heavily influenced by your environment. While you may not know exactly what you want to include in your life, it is wise to increase the size of your environment so you have more options. Remember, part and parcel of being alive is to accept that which you can't change and *grow into that which you can* — so practice making room for yourself.

TR·*ACTION*

Imagine feeling peace of mind

Pick a specific circumstance and imagine feeling deep peace of mind. Remember to include dozens of details. For example, if you are imaging yourself in a situation that involves eating, don't just see yourself comfortably eating; smell the food, taste it, hear your cup or glass when it meets the table, and notice when and how you are using your knife. Feel the chair behind you, beneath you. Notice any background sounds.

TR·*ACTION*

Learn to create the lead role in your life story

To create your custom *acting as if* movie, sit and connect to your breath until you feel your breathing settle. The more relaxed you are, the more likely your conscious mind takes a well-deserved break and allows your unconscious mind to open to suggestive *detailed* images.

Remember to include all your senses — taste, smell, touch, sight, and hearing. And remember, your subconscious does not know the difference between an imagined reality and reality itself — so make sure your movie is taking place in *present time,* not in the future.

The footlights are on, and you are in control of your story. Comfortably enter the scene, easily hit your mark, happily do whatever you wish to do, and then exit with ease.

Keep in mind that acting *as if* has nothing to do with being inauthentic and everything to do with your unconscious mind not knowing the difference between imagining and actually doing what you would like to do — all for the purpose of your being able to do the imagined — comfortably — later.

Read the following visualization entirely to understand the amount of detail I would like you to include. After reading it, close your eyes and run your own home tour.

Take several deep breaths to allow your breathing to settle. Let your belly expand on the in-breath and then collapse toward your spine on the out-breath. (Soft belly.)

Imagine someone has given you a house — maybe in the mountains or at the beach. This house will never cost you a cent nor will it involve any work. You have no responsibility but to enjoy it. A gift with no strings.

Imagine yourself standing on the street side of the house. Notice there are two doors, one in the front and one on the side covered by the roof of the carport.

Look carefully at the house. Is there a fence? How many windows do you see? Is it painted or stained? What kind of roof does it have?

Now smell the air and feel the temperature.

Listen! You can hear a dog barking a couple of houses away. You also just got a whiff of food being grilled by a neighbor, who is far away, or nearby?

Okay — start to walk toward the house, but don't go inside. Instead, walk along the side of it and notice the landscaping. Are there flowers? Foundation planting? Continue to walk along the side and, as you arrive at the back of the house, you look up and find yourself faced with a fabulous view. Stand and look at the (mountains, water, trees, or whatever you choose). Now turn and notice this side of the house. It has a porch with rocking chairs. "How nice," you think.

Now retrace your steps and go back toward the street. Walk through the door you first saw, which takes you into the kitchen. Hear your feet hit the floor as you walk on the (tile/hardwood/ linoleum) floors. Notice the color of the walls. The ceiling.

Walk over and open the refrigerator. Pull out one of the drawers.

You see cheese. Lower your head and smell the cheese. You think you also smell salami and look for it — yes, by golly, there it is — salami — under the baggie of sliced turkey. Looks totally fresh. Open the plastic wrap, pull out a piece, and taste it. Is it the old-fashioned Italian salami? As you chew the salami, close the drawer. Hear it close. Close the refrigerator door. Hear it close.

Okay, now start your own visualization of a house of your dreams.

Get into the re-runs! Before you go to sleep at night and get out of bed in the morning, get into the habit of running the movie of your new life *as if it is happening now.* When you have a few minutes to spare during the day, live your movie with your eyes wide open and rehearse how comfortable and curious you *feel.* Lastly, be sure to change the context in which you see, hear, smell, and feel yourself and your surroundings. Move from being alone to being with another to being in a group.

Once you get the hang of it, your comfort level will start to match your imagination, and your world (*with you in it*) will change for the better.

Bob's reflections on life after the death
of his wife to cancer:

Right after Margie died, I kept asking myself, "Where do I go from here, what are my options, how will I reestablish social connections, and how will I maintain my relationship with my step-children?" I wasn't sure about anything other than I would never again have sex or have a companion to share interests.

I did, however, find a wonderful partner but I was then concerned about being part of a Jewish community without a Jewish partner. Surprisingly, it hasn't been a problem at all.

I've since moved into a completely new phase of my life and am very happy. What helped most was counseling. I learned to get in touch with my feelings. Being able to have a conversation and express my feelings has helped my current relationship immensely.

COMMENTS ON THE BEST-SELLING BOOK
THE SECRET BY RHONDA BYRNE

CONTEMPORARY research confirms that we can eliminate anxiety and comfortably create change by rehearsing behavior to a point where the unconscious mind accepts the behavior as the default behavior. This concept, however, differs from the premise of the commercially successful book *The Secret*.[8] Scientific evidence does not support the book's premise that *"like attracts like;"* that is, if you think negatively, you will attract negative events to your life rather than positive events. In fact, physics confirms that *opposites* attract rather than *likes*, hence few quantum physicists support the concept behind *The Secret*.

I acknowledge that negative thinking will likely draw people of similar attitudes to you, *but this is not evidence that if you eliminate all negative thoughts, you're assured of a positive life experience.* I also acknowledge that what you focus on you amplify, a concept addressed in this chapter at length. The more you imagine having something, the better chance that you will get it.

In addition, I support Martin Seligman's evidence-based branch of psychology called *positive psychology*. It encourages individuals to acknowledge and value what is going well and focus on positive attributes and strengths they possess that will help them thrive in spite of what is going wrong.[9]

Why am I bringing up this subject? I have had several clients fear that talking about what wasn't going well would bring more disaster. With probing I often learn that the clients are using the book *The Secret* as their authority.

I remind them that they wouldn't have made the appointment if all was going well and I wonder aloud, "Since you *do* have negative thoughts, are you saying that you believe that *talking* about them will attract more negative life events?" Eventually, we find a way to discuss the problem, but it saddens me when individuals struggle to remain positive at all costs.

Let me emphasize that successful grieving depends on expressing painful emotions.

The bottom line is this: we were born with the ability to differentiate between what is going right and what is not; therefore, we will always have positive and negative thoughts. And if we become stuck emotionally, it is worthwhile to examine the factors in play, explore alternative ways of perceiving the situation, and develop effective behavior and skills to handle what can't be changed.

Lastly, I believe little good comes from insisting that we create 100 percent of our personal reality, especially when it comes to disease. While we need to remain alert to environmental and behavioral reasons for disease, let's remember that a human's normal life cycle is one of birth to death. In our desire to defy death, we often place a subtle shame on individuals who become ill. This is unfortunate for everyone involved. Even when lifestyle choices do contribute to manifesting a terminal illness, showing kindness after the fact is always better than placing blame.

Notes

1. Siegel, Dan (2010). *Mindsight: the new science of personal transformation*. New York: Bantam Books. p. 6.
2. Garfield, Charles (1984). *Athletes*. New York: Warner Books. p. 16.
3. Doidge, M.D., Norman (2007). *The Brain That Changes Itself*. New York: Penguin Books. p. 84.
4. Yapko, Michael (2012). *Trancework: An Introduction to the Practice of Clinical Hypnosis*. 4th Ed. New York: Routledge. p. 18.
5. Gaillard R., Del Cul, A., Naccache, L., et al. (2006). Nonconscious semantic processing of emotional words modulates conscious access. *Proc. Natl Acad, Sci. USA*. 103(19): 7524–9:7524–9. doi:10.1073/pnas.0600584103; Greenwald, A. G., Draine, S. C., and Abrams, R. L. (1996). Three cognitive markers of unconscious semantic activation. *Science* 273 (5282): 1699–702. doi:10.1126/science; Kiefer, M., and Brendel, D. (February 2006). Attentional modulation of unconscious "automatic" processes: evidence from event-related potentials in a masked priming paradigm. *J Cogn Neurosci* 18 (2): 184–98. doi:10.1162/089892906775783688; Naccache, L., Gaillard, R., Adam, C. et al. (May 2005). A direct intracranial record of emotions evoked by subliminal words. *Proc. Natl. Acad. Sci U.S.A.* 102 (21): 7713–7. doi:10.1073/pnas.0500542102.
6. Langer, E. J. (1989). *Mindfulness*. Reading, MA: Addison Wesley.
7. Fritz, Robert (2002). *Your Life as Art*. Robert Fritz Inc. p. 191.
8. Byrne, Rhonda (2006). *The Secret*. New York: Atria Books.
9. Seligman, Martin, Steen, Tracy, and Park, Nansook. Positive psychology progress: empirical validation of interventions. http://www.ebt.org/files/empiricaldata.pdf.

CHAPTER TWELVE

Love Aside:
"New Relationship" Facts and Figures

*Romance is thinking about your significant other when you
are supposed to be thinking about something else.*

— Nicholas Sparks

How many photos are too many?

ONE OF the most charming questions I ever received in
class came from a middle-aged man named Sam. He said,
"If I were to invite a woman over to dinner, how many
framed pictures of my deceased wife would be too many?"

Everyone laughed, but his question was a good one. Sam, like
most people who have lost a mate, had increased the number of
framed photos around his house so he could feel his late wife's
presence. I answered his question with one of my own: "If you
went into a widow's home, how many photos of her deceased
spouse would it take for you to feel uncomfortable?" He laughed
and said it was time to dismantle the shrine.

Because the class had been meeting for months, a few of the
women felt comfortable enough to tease Sam about starting to
date. He went along with it for a while, and then said he didn't
consider the woman he invited for dinner a date, nor did he think
she would consider herself a date. Sam explained how much he

missed having a meaningful conversation with the opposite sex. "Besides," he said, "I'm simply doing what Vicki reminds us to do after each session: 'Don't forget! Practice connecting!'"

Yes, Sam had been listening. He perceived his upcoming dinner as an opportunity to have a meaningful conversation with a woman. Practicing would allow him to develop a level of comfort for when he did meet a woman he wanted to date.

The touchy subject of dating

In *The Creative Habit*, choreographer Twyla Tharp describes how we stifle creative living when we insist on believing that certain things are true *or* false and right *or* wrong rather than considering something could be true *as well as* false and right *as well as* wrong.[1] This doesn't apply to illegal or immoral acts but, rather, to how different family and ethnic cultures have different perspectives about right and wrong. How often do you forget that you are talking about what is personally true or false, right or wrong, for *you*? Can you remember an instance when you changed your mind about what you once thought was right or wrong?

To determine if a belief is *absolutely* wrong, Tharp challenges you to identify ways in which the opposite can also be true. She contends that you are open-minded and free to live creatively when you understand that, quite often, *neither is right or wrong because both are right and wrong*. Relax and remember that experts are usually those who determine societal right and wrong — and experts don't agree!

For example, you might say that you are not interested in a committed relationship because you are not interested in being a caregiver again. However, that same relationship can become a positive when you think about another person caring and supporting *you*.

Let me list a few of my own observations about people

starting new relationships.

- When the building of a relationship is rushed, it often fails, throwing the individual back into a grief cycle. In class I draw a round peg in a square hole on the white board to remind people that a round peg can be put into a square hole if you make the round peg small enough. In other words, you can make yourself fit into someone else's world even when it isn't a good fit for you over the long term. But does that sound appealing?

- When I offer to snap my fingers and guarantee that everyone in the room is in a committed relationship with a financially stable, even-tempered, handy, healthy, loving, humorous, generous partner — someone who loves to cook and garden — and will graciously care for and outlive her or him, and then ask the class how many would refuse — no one raises their hand.

- The thought of dating can be paralyzing, but seldom do people understand that it is sometimes more the fear of dating than the idea of a relationship that scares them.

- Many who insist they are not going to date change their minds immediately after meeting someone interesting.

- A few individuals strongly believe it is morally wrong to commit to another relationship. If you wrestle with thinking you should remain alone because of your prior commitment, review the traditional wedding vows:

  To have and to hold
  From this day forward.
  For better, for worse,
  For richer, for poorer,
  In sickness and in health,
  To love and to cherish
  Till death do us part.

Wisely, no restrictions were placed on how to live your life after you completed your vows.

- No matter what you know you want or don't want, expect people to talk to you about dating. Try to understand and be kind. Now that you are without a companion, it is normal for others to think you might be interested in another relationship.

- Know that there is absolutely nothing wrong with you if you are not interested in committing to a new relationship. Period.

The void created by "not belonging to another"

Issues about no longer belonging to another and feeling a lack of purpose often come up in the first months of classes. When I ask people to explain what they mean, they often say that "there's no reason to make an effort because there's no one around to appreciate it." This response is common when we are talking about the need to eat a decent meal instead of snacking. Initially, people complain about shopping and cooking for one person, but ultimately someone says, "It is not the shopping or prep, it's about not having someone to share the food once it's prepared."

Our social connections remind us of our value, and research supports that those of us who are socially connected are healthier, have fewer stress-related problems, and recover from trauma and illness faster.[2] Yet many widows and widowers are reticent to seek a new partner because the quality of the relationship, after commitment, is uncertain. Occasionally, a class member is brave enough to express her apprehension by saying, "What happens if I remarry and find I'm unhappier than I was living alone?" It's a good question and a valid concern.

However, I recently sent a questionnaire to 90 widows and

widowers I have worked with over the years. Of the 60 percent who responded, more than half are happily remarried or in a committed relationship. Many reported that their current relationship was more loving and rewarding than the one they had with their deceased mate.

You are never too old to love and be loved

Recently, a 92-year-old man named Ed joined one of my groups. As the months progressed, he pulled me aside to say he felt guilty returning for the next session because he was "too happy." I wasn't surprised that Ed was doing well because, even though he had a severe hearing problem, he was very active and played bridge and doubles tennis every week. As I listened, something about his smile made me suspect he was dating and, in fact, he went on to say that he was. His question for me was "Do you think I'm rushing things?" Instead of answering, I asked if he would be willing to talk about his situation with the group. Reluctantly, he agreed.

As the group conversation started, Ed shyly announced he wouldn't be returning because he didn't feel right coming to report that he was happy. He explained that he and his deceased wife had been close friends with another couple and often traveled together. The man had died, and Ed had recently met the widowed wife for breakfast. A few days later, they met for lunch and found they were still together for dinner. Now, he said, they spend every day together. Interestingly, he ended by saying, "You know, my grown children have been very supportive, but they just don't 'do it for me.'" Ed turned and again asked me, "Do you think I'm rushing it?" Having gauged the group's response from the expressions on their faces, I said, "Considering how well you know each other and your age, I wouldn't change a thing." After a short pause, the group broke into applause and provided additional encouragement.

Granted, Ed's story seems exceptional considering his age, but my grandmother also entered into a relationship after being widowed at age 88. Because she was in good health, she was able to live alone in an apartment complex with other elderly men and women. One of the men scheduled lunch dates with my grandmother. Before long, they were spending entire days together until his daughter moved him across town to a cheaper apartment. Still, he came over every Wednesday to visit my grandmother, making two bus connections across Tucson, stopping at Wendy's on his way to pick up burgers for their lunch.

At age 92, my grandmother moved into an assisted living facility, and I forgot about the gentleman who had been so good to her. When she died at 96, we planned a small, simple graveside service because all of her friends had predeceased her. As the minister started to speak, I noticed a man using a walker coming across the large expanse of grass toward us. Instantly, I knew who he was. I stopped the minister and went to meet the man. Together, we slowly walked back to the tent that shaded my grandmother's casket. I hadn't cried that day — until I saw him place his hand on Jennie's casket.

Ed and my grandmother are not the exceptions. Mark Brooks, who tracks dating services, reports a double-digit increase in seniors using online dating service since 2003; however, *remarriage rates have not increased.*[3] Demographer Susan Brown of Ohio's Bowling Green State University found that full-time cohabiting among older people increased 50 percent, based on census figures from 2000 to 2005, while part-time cohabiting increased as well.[4]

Reconnecting with high school and college friends
Nancy was a 36-year-old class member whose husband had

had a fatal heart attack during an early morning run. His death left her raising three children under the age of eight.

Months after her group's class ended, I received an email from another member saying Nancy had reconnected with an old boyfriend in Arizona. I had to give Nancy credit. Still, I wondered how many men would want to "inherit" three very young children. A year later, I ran into another class member at the grocery store, and she said that Nancy had married her old boyfriend. Apparently the man loved children, but he and his ex-wife were childless when they divorced. What a gift. He was not only still in love with Nancy; he was thrilled to father her three young children as well.

Margie was in her 50s and had been in a lesbian relationship for 25 years until her partner died of cancer. She moved through the raw pain of her loss but was extremely lonely. One evening she shared that a friend encouraged her to connect to old high school and college friends on Facebook. She decided against it because none of them knew she was a lesbian. With time, however, Margie opened a Facebook account and found that writing to her old classmates was a kick. As the online conversations continued, she told them that she was lesbian and that her long-time lover had passed away the year before. The response to her post was overwhelmingly positive. The bonus came when one of her classmates said she also was lesbian and lived within an hour's drive of Margie. Before long, they were meeting weekly for dinner.

Watching people connect, I became intrigued enough to look for research on the subject. To my surprise, Nancy Kalish, a developmental psychologist, was spurred by her own reconnection to a former high school boyfriend to conduct a large survey of others who had reconnected.

Kalish surveyed 1001 people who reconnected with their old

flames, then wrote the book, *Lost and Found Lovers.*[5] Here are a few intriguing results from her "lost love project":

- Of the rekindled first loves, 84 percent were younger than 22 when they first fell in love. Another 10 percent were ages 23 to 29, and 62 percent of them were first loves.
- Many of the original relationships lasted several years.
- A great many of the relationships ended because of parental disapproval.
- Couples who had been parted the longest had the highest chance of remaining together.
- The stay-together rate of rekindled relationships was extremely high (72 percent) and even higher (78 percent) for the couples who were each other's first loves.
- Only six percent reconnected after a class reunion.
- One couple got back together after 55 years of separation.
- Some were ill, but that didn't stop them from rekindling their relationship.

It seems to be a universal truth: if you once felt something special when connecting to another, you never forget the person.

Missed Connections on craigslist

In looking further into the concept of missed connections, I discovered that craigslist has *Missed Connection* groups — specific to locale. The postings are sometimes funny, usually heartwarming, and often bittersweet. Sadly, craigslist retires the posts after they've been online for only a week.

The Australian artist Sophie Blackall became so inspired by the craigslist messages that she collected her favorite posts and turned them into a series of paintings, which led to the book *Missed Connections: Love, Lost & Found.*[6] Each post in the book is accompanied by a zany and unforgettable illustration.

With Blackall's permission, I am including one of the craigslist posts here:

The Whale at Coney Island—M4—Age 69 (Brooklyn)

A young friend of mine recently acquainted me with the intricacies of Missed Connections, *and I have decided to try to find you one final time.*

Many years ago, we were friends and teachers together in New York City. Perhaps we could have been lovers too, but we were not. We used to take trips to Coney Island, especially during the spring, when we would stroll hand in hand, until our palms got too sweaty, along the boardwalk, and take refuge in the cool darkness of the aquarium. We liked to visit the whale best. One spring, it arrived from its winter home (in Florida? I can't remember) pregnant. Everyone at the aquarium was very excited — a baby beluga whale was going to be born in New York City! You insisted that we not miss the birth, so every day after class, and on both Saturday and Sunday, we would take the D train all the way from Harlem to Coney Island.

We got there one Saturday as the aquarium opened and there was a sign posted to the glass tank. The baby beluga had been born dead. The mother, the sign read, was recovering but would be fine. We read the sign in shock and watched the single beluga whale in her tank. She was circling slowly. Neither of us could speak. Suddenly, without warning, the beluga started to throw herself against the wall of the tank. Trainers came and ushered us out. We sat on a bench outside, and suddenly I felt tears running down my face. You saw, turned my face towards yours, and kissed me. We had never kissed before, and I let my lips linger on yours for a second before I stood up and walked towards the ocean.

Are you out there, dear friend? If so, please respond. I think of you often.

The biggest surprise for Blackall was receiving 27 emails from couples who had reunited as a result of the *Missed Connections* website group.

Starting a relationship with children living at home

Death anxiety can be particularly high when an individual has school-aged children at home. When I ask surviving parents to prioritize what they need to do to manage their family, inevitably I am told "stay alive until I get the kids through school."

This parental priority, however, often manifests as an anxious overbearing need for control, and the home environment can become unbearable as a result. When this happens, the kids flee the house in order to emotionally breathe. My job (and in this particular scenario, I often fail) is to help the remaining parent refocus on living rather than worrying about dying. I typically stress the importance of opening my clients' home(s) to people of both sexes and all ages as soon as possible.

To those readers who have school-aged children: Yes, I realize you are exhausted. Yes, I know that you can barely get your kids to school on time, let alone maintain a clean house. So what do you do? Well, forget the house and encourage people whom your children don't know well to occasionally stop by your messy home for short drop-in visits.

Why do I suggest this? First, it is important to create an environment filled with *the living*. Second, having your kids meet new people on a regular basis is good practice for when you later introduce them to someone you'd like to date. If you haven't witnessed a child sabotage a relationship that could be good for you and them, delay exposing your children to adult friends until it is time to introduce them to a *special friend*. If they aren't used to having your adult friends in their home prior to the introduction, don't expect to be pleased by their response.

As casual as you might try to be, they aren't used to meeting new people and will assume the person is destined to replace their deceased parent.

Bottom line — to prevent your children from overreacting later, ask for help now. Let your friends know that you want your children to become comfortable with both men and women dropping by for a cup of coffee, a glass of wine, or a pizza dinner with the family. It is not unusual for children to develop a good relationship with an adult of the opposite sex — that is, if they don't feel pressured. In fact, children often surprise a parent by suggesting he or she date someone they have gotten to know and like.

If your children are in high school and soon to graduate, it could be wise to delay dating. But if they're younger, what do you consider a reasonable delay — a few years, a decade? (Note: Helen Fisher's research[7] indicates couples face fewer problems if the children are grade school age at the time of a remarriage.)

In any case, keep in mind that the decision to remarry is *yours*, not your children's. If your new partner is willing to move through the five to seven years it takes to create solid family relationships and you are up for supporting your new mate, then everyone can benefit from a two-parent home.

Psychotherapist and stepmom Sue Thoele gives a clear picture of what remarriage with children can entail in her book, *The Courage to Be a Stepmom.*[8] She points out that because your new relationship was born out of loss, you can expect a child's grieving for the deceased parent to be rekindled when a stepmother or stepfather moves into the home.

Therefore, it is important to talk to your new partner about not doing *too much too soon*. It is even better if you role-play different family scenarios and specifically agree on how you will discipline and handle certain decisions.

To keep the marriage intact, Thoele suggests that new couples work with a therapist who specializes in stepparenting issues. She also urges the new partner to join a stepparent group to gain support and feedback as to when to assert themselves and how to detach when something isn't about them.

Remarriage when there are adult children

A remarriage with grown children can also present problems before and during the marriage — as well as after the remaining parent's death — when the children often abruptly end contact with the stepparent.

Unfortunately, there is seldom enough face time for the adult children and new partner to develop a close, caring relationship. The situation can be improved if the biological parent is willing to have a few upfront conversations with his or her children. The new relationship is also less likely to be ruptured if the new couple doesn't carry high expectations of the children.

Here's a good example of a bad start. Bill first came to see me because he was anxious about dating. We met on a regular basis as he started to pursue online dating. After he had dated several women, he felt he was on his way and our sessions ended.

About a year after our first meeting, he called and asked me to meet with him and the woman he was planning to marry. He said he wanted to clear up a problem before they flew East to see his son. When I told him I didn't work with couples, he reminded me of my specialty — life transitions. Cornered, I took out my calendar to book an appointment.

Bill and Mary came in the next week and settled in side by side on the sofa. I opened by saying, "So, Mary, I understand you're meeting Bill's son next week?" Bill's face became pained, and Mary clearly didn't intend to speak. Finally, Bill explained that Mary had insisted on speaking to his son on the telephone recently, and it hadn't gone well. Since then, he and Mary had been arguing because she felt Bill's son had been rude and disrespectful to her on the phone.

Bill said that he had warned Mary to tread lightly during her phone conversation with his son, but she said, "Don't worry. I know what I am doing. You will see. I will win your son over before you know it!"

As Bill completed his sentence, Mary started to talk. The problem started when she told Bill's son that she was looking forward to merging the two families and being called "Grandma" by Bill's newborn grandchild. Apparently Bill's son had trouble responding to her request, which caused Mary to try to convince him. Considering the baby was not a month old and she had yet to meet the son, I thought the son's response was appropriate: "Why don't we wait and see how it goes. I'm sure we can work something out that everyone will agree to as time goes on."

After reporting the phone conversation, Mary looked at me for support, saying she couldn't believe he'd say something like that to her. I told Mary I understood her desire to become part of the family. And because she was divorced, I also understood her thinking that the families would merge in some fashion as they often do after a divorce — with everyone becoming a full-fledged member of the extended family. That said, I suggested she not compare grown children's responses to the death of a parent as similar to how they'd respond if their two living parents divorced.

I wondered aloud if she could initially focus on being a friend to Bill's son and his family. It was obvious from the expression on her face that she didn't like my suggestion. Finally, I asked if she was up for testing the worst case scenario: if a friendship wasn't allowed to slowly develop with Bill's son, she might find herself being asked to stay at home while her husband visited his son's family without her.

She didn't see that as an option and I wasn't about to argue, but I told her I thought she was in for rough times unless she changed her approach. I never heard how the trip went or how the marriage is working. Hopefully, Bill has not had to choose between his new wife and his son.

If you are in this situation, understand that even in a best-case scenario, it is almost a given that *your grown children will initially be uncomfortable with your new partner*. The first hurdle they must clear is accepting that your new relationship doesn't mean that you have stopped caring for their deceased parent.

If you are planning to make a permanent commitment, schedule time to talk with each of your children one-on-one — without your new partner nearby. Express your appreciation for how they are coping with the new situation. Acknowledge that, on the one hand, they have to be uncomfortable with the new arrangement but, on the other hand, maybe they will feel relieved you are no longer lonely and unhappy. By giving them a way to "hold the contradiction," they may hold their tongues as well.

If your children try to squelch the relationship or treat you like a child every time you speak of it, put boundaries in place immediately. Kindly let them know you are proceeding in spite of their objections, and that you hope, over time, they will learn to enjoy your new companion. When they realize they can't derail the relationship, they will likely go back to leading their own lives.

Additional hot buttons

Your children's discomfort will be especially acute if they see your new partner living in the home you shared with their deceased parent. If there are no financial constraints, the two of you might consider moving into a new place that holds no memories for the children.

If you do remain in the home you shared with your deceased partner and decide to remodel, many grown children will view such expenditures as money taken from their inheritance. In anticipation of their concern, visit your estate planner, create a prenuptial agreement, and tell your children about it. That way, your children know the family's assets won't be inherited by your new partner.

Last, be prepared to lose some of your old "couple" friends because of their loyalty to your deceased partner. This might not make any sense, but it happens often. Also realize your new partner may be uncomfortable around your old friends for fear of being compared to your late spouse.

Research on seniors remarrying

Deborah Carr of Rutgers University conducted a study[9] of widows and widowers over the age of 65. Her results were summarized in the *Journal of Marriage and Family* in 2004 this way:

- Many widows prefer their independence over the benefits of companionship.
- Even though widowers are more concerned about being desirable due to old age and ill health, they are more prepared to take a chance on a new relationship than widows.
- Individuals are more likely to start dating six months after the death of their partner if there was prior marital conflict.
- Eighteen months after the death, having strong social support reduces men's desire to remarry by 70 percent and women's by 30 percent.
- Homemaking or home repair skills are not motivators for dating or the desire to remarry.
- More than 60 percent of men but less than 20 percent of women are involved in a new romance or remarried after two years of being widowed.

- Surviving spouses who remarry have more positive outcomes, such as greater life satisfaction and less depression, than single widows and widowers. Further research shows that the reduced depression is due to the remarried individuals' higher household incomes and less anxiety over financial matters. If finances are not a problem, there's no difference in levels of depression between spouses who remarry and those who don't.

Keep in mind that no one wants to follow a saint

It is common to *forget what you didn't like* about your deceased partner and your relationship and *amplify what you did like.* This can lead to a kind of nostalgic sainthood that no one wants to follow. Therefore, stay in touch with reality — that is, when you and your new partner start to squabble, catch yourself before you drift into remembering your previous relationship as being trouble-free.

Weighing the finances before deciding to remarry

If you decide to remarry, be sure to talk to an accountant about the financial pros and cons first. If you are retired, you may not be able to afford losing your share of your deceased spouse's social security. Depending on finances, you may decide to remain unmarried and cohabitate or become LAT companions (Living Apart Together — a new term for intimate ongoing companions who maintain independent households).

Post-it® dating

If you are dating, I suggest using Post-its® to write down a one- or two-word impression after each date — prior to sexual intimacy. It is uncanny how sexual intimacy causes you to ignore obvious incompatibility issues. In fact, sexual intimacy can cause you to initially overlook what you can't later tolerate.

Here are a few sample Post-it® impressions:

Rude	Impulsive
Courteous	Indecisive
Kind	Drinks too much
Sharp-tongued	Boring
Thoughtful	Talks too much
Thoughtless	Never talks
Gentle	Narcissistic
Rough	Pleaser
Generous	Insecure
Selfish	Secure
Self-centered, self-absorbed	Loud
Well-balanced	Quiet
Considerate	Sensitive
Narrow-minded	Insensitive
Open-minded	Distant
Curious	Loving/warm
Set in their ways	Cold/undemonstrative
Easygoing	Controlling
Hot-tempered	Flexible

Recently, a woman wrote a note to thank me for suggesting the Post-it® dating idea. She was close to committing to a relationship when she remembered to review her Post-it dating notes. She was both surprised and saddened when reading her one- and and two-word impressions, but she was wise enough to end the relationship. Even better news: she's currently in a healthy and satisfying committed relationship.

TR·*ACTION*

1. Write what you have to gain and what you have to lose by remaining on your own.

GAIN   **LOSE**

What do you specifically like about living alone?

What do you dislike?

2. Next, consider what you have to gain and what you have to lose by committing to another person.

GAIN   **LOSE**

What specifically do you like about being in a relationship?

What do you dislike?

3. Is there another way of getting what you need?

Nancy's reflections on life after her husband died shortly after heart surgery:

Being alone with three teenagers was the worst part. Losing a father and becoming a teenager is a bad combination. My eldest son became a terror, and thankfully I was able to get him out of a bad environment and into a rural setting for a year. My second son became explosive, and my daughter had to deal with it all. I felt like I was in the middle of a war. I had to get my children through their grief before I could focus on mine.

I didn't think I could handle my grief, my kids' grief, and my husband's professional affairs, medical bills, and financial planning — by myself. But I learned how to lean on neighbors and my "real" friends when the chips were down.

I still feel guilty about taking my husband for granted and the spats we got into. Surprisingly I have become closer to my eldest son, closer than I would have ever thought possible. Plus, I thought I'd never be interested in another mate, but I have started to date occasionally.

Notes

1. Tharp, Twyla (2005). *The Creative Habit.* New York: Simon & Schuster.
2. Diener, Ed, and Biswas-Diener, Robert (2008). *Happiness.* Boston: Wiley-Blackwell; 1st edition.
3. Brooks, Mark. http://www.mcclatchydc.com/2008/07/16/v-print/44481/as-seniors-live-longer-they-find.html.
4. Brown, S., Bulanda, J.R., Lee, G. (2005). The significance of nonmarital cohabitation: Marital status and mental health benefits among middle-aged and older adults. *J Gerontol B Psychol Sci Soc Sci* (2005) 60 (1): S21-S29. doi:10.1093/geronb/60.1.S21.
5. Kalish, Nancy (1997). *Lost and Found Lovers: Facts and fantasies of rekindled romances.* New York: William Morrow.

6. Blackall, Sophie (2011). *Missed Connections: Love, Lost & Found.* New York: Workman Publishing.
7. Fisher, Helen (1994). *Anatomy of Love.* New York: Ballantine.
8. Theole, Sue Patton (2011). *The Courage to Be a Stepmom: Finding Your Place without Losing Yourself.* E-Book/Amazon.
9. Carr, Deborah (2004). The desire to date and remarry among older widows and widowers, *Journal of Marriage and Family.* 66, 1051–1068.

CHAPTER THIRTEEN

Four Magic Questions
You Will Thank Me for Asking

*There is no one out there to save us, to take care of us, to heal the hurt.
But there is a very fine person within, one we barely know, ready and
willing to be our constant companion.*

— Hollis, *Middle Life*

CHARLES JOHNSON writes in *Necessary Wisdom* that "in pausing and listening within I am not just noticing what is within; I am, in ways I can never fully comprehend, participating in creating what is within."[1] This quote beautifully defines the process I call "simmering."

Simmering is the slow process of piecing together partially formed thoughts and images as they bubble up. It is the stuff of Post-its and the internal process of creation. It is also the process of accepting that on a certain day you can still feel weaker than you ever expected and the next day feel stronger than you ever thought possible.

"God gives every bird a worm, but won't throw [the worm] into the nest."

This Swedish proverb hits the nail on the head, doesn't it? You have learned that your life is not over, but to live it fully you must leave your nest to get what you want and need.

When I help clients decide what their new lifestyle will include, we commence by working with the following key questions:

- What do I want to include in my life?
- What do I never want to include in my life?
- What do I have now that I would like to eliminate?
- What do I have now that I want to keep?

The first question may seem quite simple but, in reality, people find it difficult to specifically articulate what they want. Women in particular have a hard time defining what they want because many have been preoccupied with filling others' needs. One widow said to me, "What? What do *I* want? No one has ever asked me that before!"

Whether it is difficult to conceive of what you would really like to include in your life or simply hard to admit, answering the remaining three questions above will help you indirectly arrive at the answer to your primary question. Keep in mind that while you may have physical limitations, it doesn't mean you must think of yourself as handicapped, and while you may have financial limitations, it doesn't mean you can't find joy in the precious parts of life that are inexpensive and often free.

To help you understand exactly how your answers to the last three questions will apply to your answering your main question, let me walk you through a sample step-by-step process. Don't make the mistake of assuming that the following lists should be your lists. They shouldn't. You are unique and your lists should be as well.

1. **First pass:** List what comes to mind and don't be concerned about repetition.

What I don't want to include in my life:

Job I dislike	Sadness
Fear	Loneliness

What do I have that I want to eliminate?

Fear	Negative attitude
Sadness	Guilt
Anger	Disorganization
Instability	Need to please others
Loneliness	Reclusive lifestyle
Lack of focus	Car that doesn't work
Inflexibility	Physically out of shape

What do I have that I want to keep?

Friends	Faith
Family	Dog
House	

2. **Second pass:** Convert your answers to the last three questions into a "what I want" format (shown below in italics).

What I don't want to include in my life

Job I dislike – *job I like*
Sadness – *happiness*
Fear – *bravery*
Loneliness – *people/activities*

What do I have in my life that I want to eliminate?

Fear – *bravery*
Sadness – *happiness/humor*
Anger – *peace*
Instability – *stability*
Loneliness – *people and activities with other people*
Lack of focus – *focus*
Inflexibility – *flexibility*
Negative attitude – *positive attitude*
Guilt – *guilt-free*
Disorganization – *organization*
Need to please others – *please myself*
Reclusive lifestyle – *active life*
Car that doesn't work – *new, different car*
Physically out of shape – *get physically in shape*

What do I have in my life that I want to keep?

Friends – *friends*   Faith – *faith*
Family – *family*   Dog – *dog*
House – *house*

3. **Third pass:** Consolidate what is repetitious and create your *What I want to include in my life* list.

What I want to include in my life

Friends	Focus
Family	Flexibility
Good health	Positive guilt-free brave attitude
Financial stability	No need for another's approval
Job/volunteering I like	Active life
Peace and contentment	Faith

Activities/interests	Dog
Stability	House

4. **Check for life balance:** Look at your final list as it pertains to the following eight categories. Is there something you would like to add to your list that would provide balance?

Spirituality/Nature	Health
Career/Volunteering	Personal Growth
Fun/Recreation	Significant Other/Romance
Money	Friends and Family

5. **Check your Post-it® notes:** Gather your Post-it® notes and see if you have written down something that should be on your final list. For example, one of my clients added the following: play a drum, take photography class, and go to a different church each Sunday.

6. **Group similar items and then prioritize your list:** Group similar traits, feelings, and activities and then *prioritize your list by putting numbers in the left margin.*

7. **Create a clean copy of your list with prioritized entries.**

Commit to a plan of action

With your list balanced and prioritized, it is time to shift *from thinking* about what you want *to envisioning yourself taking action.* To avoid being overwhelmed, start by committing to *one thing* each week that will bring you closer to your having what you want — *that you don't currently have.* Granted, many things on your list will require a certain sequence of behavior, so be specific: list the steps that will be necessary, imagine moving through the steps successfully and then start to take action.

Also ask yourself what could interfere, and then consider how you might prevent that from happening. Once you *see* yourself preventing future interference — you are prepared for it.

If you find yourself making something difficult that is actually easy, recognize that you are *closing down and turning in* again. Stop right there, *clear your head, open up and remember you have the ability to tolerate anything for a short time.*

Being busy is no excuse

In the months following your partner's death, being busy served you well, but *there is a big difference between being busy and being active.* Being active includes a sense of purpose.

To make sure you have time to be active, review the "must do" list you carry around in your head — the one that propels you forward without thinking. How long has it been since you questioned what is genuinely urgent? Put another way, how often do you put your life on hold to take care of something you treat as urgent — that isn't?

Take time right now to list and label what you do that is 1) necessary, 2) urgent, and 3) habitual. Think carefully about it. What can be eliminated entirely?

I realize this chapter might seem counterintuitive to learning and living sideways, but it isn't. You are simply defining *what matters for you now* and then developing a way to get it. What you discover living on the slant will be a bonus and fodder for when you update your "living document" as you move forward.

Shirley's reflections on life after her husband died of emphysema:

Because we lived for two years knowing Paul would die, I didn't think I would have such a difficult time after his death, but I found I was filled with resentment.

I resented not having someone to back me up. I resented having to be solely responsible. I resented having to be an adult — grown up! But what I resented most was my husband not taking care of himself. His death could have been delayed for years.

Looking for a new partner was a big hurdle. I never expected to again love so deeply. Instead, I have found a greater love with fewer surprises.

I went back to work and have gotten my "self" back. I no longer care what people think of me. I won't let someone else's narrow frame of reference deter me from dreaming a bigger life.

Notes

1. Johnson, M.D., Charles (1991). *Necessary Wisdom*. Berkeley CA: Celestial Arts. pp. 196–7.

CHAPTER FOURTEEN

On Track for A Life of Your Own

We must be willing to give up the life we've planned,
so as to have the life that is waiting for us.
— Joseph Campbell

Only you know what isn't wrong with your life

IN THE months immediately following your loved one's death, you were forced to focus on simply surviving. Inevitably time moves you beyond basic survival to a place where you can feel the pain of loss, but suffering is becoming optional. If you are at that place, it is time to stop and ask yourself, "What in my life isn't wrong?"

In a recent interview on National Public Radio[1], comedian Joan Rivers talked about recovering from the death of her husband Edgar and the financial collapse that came with it. She ended the interview by saying, "Faced with the aftermath of tragedy, we forget to consider what is going right. We just don't know when we're lucky."

If you read the local newspaper or listen to the six o'clock news, you know that "what bleeds leads." If there is something to be savored from listening to the news, it is this: whatever horror happened, it didn't happen to you! For example, yesterday you entered an intersection 30 seconds before a serious accident took place. Someone's car was towed, but thankfully it wasn't yours.

A tornado dipped down and tore through four city blocks, but it didn't hit your home. Because it didn't, you are faced with what *hasn't gone wrong* and how you are going to live with *what is going right.*

Getting to the core of your inner strength

There is a wonderful story in Ashley Davis Bush's book, *Transcending Loss*[2], about a famous old apple tree in New Hampshire that produces more fruit than any other tree in the area. One assumes this tree was well-tended, but, in truth, its trunk was deeply scarred from a bolt of lightning and the swing of an axe, probably in an attempt to cut it down entirely. Yet, despite the onslaught, this apple tree not only survived its hardships, but each year since it shows its strength of purpose by providing more fruit than expected.

Like the apple tree, we each have the creative potential to adapt to the hardship that interrupts our life, and ultimately rally to live with a sense of purpose.

Three good things

There have been dozens of research projects on happiness. Of all of the methods tested over an extended period, an exercise called "Three Good Things" has been shown to be the most effective.

In the original study[3], psychologists Peterson and Seligman asked participants to list three things that went well each day and to reflect on why they happened. They noted a significant shift away from negative feelings to a positive sense of optimism and well-being at the one-month mark and an additional boost at three months. At six months, the "Three Good Things" exercise exceeded all other methods being tested.

In general terms, happiness is an elusive concept, but it is important to accept that general well-being and contentment can remain stable in both good and bad times.[4] You can feel sad while maintaining a sense of contentment, you can have bittersweet memories of the past and simultaneously create positive future memories.

In Chapter Twelve, you started to track what you want and don't want to include in your future. The process encourages you to act in your best interest. In accepting that you can be *at cause* rather than only *at effect,* you reinforce the belief that you deserve a full and rewarding life. This belief loops back and continues to remind you to envision yourself having what you want and then taking action.

Never forget:
Your emotional foundation is made up of people

Being from the Midwest, I was taught that a tree's roots generally go as deep as its branches go high. I was surprised to learn that is not the case for the magnificent towering California redwood. It not only lacks a deep tap root, but its root system seldom grows deeper than six feet below the surface. Considering how top-heavy a redwood becomes at maturity, how does it survive? The answer: its lateral root system intertwines with the root systems of adjacent trees for stability. Isn't this how a group of close friends function for each other as well?

Rebecca Adams, a professor of sociology, says that friendship makes a bigger impact on psychological well-being than family relationships.[5] Her research also found that the amount of contact or proximity is not as critical as simply knowing support is available if and when it is needed. In addition, a review of 150 studies showed that individuals with strong social ties had a 50 percent better chance of survival — regardless of age, sex, and health status.[6]

There is no doubt about it: the wider the range of people you befriend, the more stable your emotional foundation. So think carefully before rejecting a potential friend. Step back and remember that each person you meet has something different to offer.

To broaden your view of friendship, keep the following in mind:

- Develop different kinds of friendships depending on the activities you share.
- Don't be put off if a friend doesn't share all of your preferences.
- Allow a new friendship to grow as it will or won't.
- Allow an existing friendship to change. It can be just as good but different.
- Invest time in rewarding relationships; limit your time with those that are emotionally draining.

Whenever you hear yourself say, "I can't do that," ask yourself if you mean you don't want to do it. "I can't" is often an excuse and a signal that a competing commitment is running the show. For example:

"I want to have dinner with "so and so" but I can't, because what I want more is to feel safe and comfortable. If I ask and they accept I'd have to cope with not feeling smart enough, or entertaining enough to be a good dinner partner."

The previous self-talk example may sound humorous, but it is truly the way our minds work. *Consider how a little upfront anxiety will ultimately allow you to have more friends and therefore feel safer in the long run.*

Cultivate a few close confidants

In her TED talk, social researcher Brene Brown reminds us that we are neurobiologically wired for deep connection: when asked about love, we talk about heartbreak; when asked about belonging, we talk about exclusion. In a nutshell, when asked about connection, we tell stories of disconnection.

In trying to ascertain what it takes to deeply connect to another, Brown concluded that we must be willing to be vulnerable. To do that well, we have to let go of *who we think we should be so that we can become who we really are.* It is not an easy or pleasant undertaking for many of us, but as Bob Dylan's lyric says: *"He not busy being born is busy dying."*[7]

Care for yourself by caring for others

Psychologist Bill O'Hanlon[8] provides a beautiful example of how you can enrich your own life — and the lives of others — if you concentrate on what you *can do* and what you *like to do.*

Milton Erickson, the famous physician and psychiatrist, was asked to visit a colleague's widowed aunt while Erickson was in Milwaukee on business. The elderly aunt had few living relatives and used a wheelchair because of ill health. During the colleague's last phone conversation with his aunt, she hinted that life was no longer worth living. This concerned him. Erickson agreed to see her and called her in advance to say he would stop by for a visit.

As Erickson entered the woman's house, he noticed the draperies were closed and little had been done to the interior for decades. After a short tour of the house, the woman took him to her greenhouse where she spent hours making African violet cuttings for later repotting.

Since being confined to a wheelchair, she confided that she only ventured out to church on Sundays when her handyman drove her to the church, lifted her into a pew, and returned to help her out after the service ended.

After listening to her tale, Erickson explained that her nephew thought she might be depressed, but he disagreed. He didn't think depression was her problem. Instead, he thought her difficulty stemmed from not being a good Christian. Obviously, this took her by surprise, but undaunted, he told her specifically what she should do to become a better Christian.

First, she should get more African violet slips started. Next, she should comb the church membership list and each Sunday's bulletin for birthdates, illness, engagements, marriages, funerals — any happy or sad event in the life of a church member. Then for each occasion, she should put a violet into a gift pot and have her handyman drive her to the family's home, where she would offer her plant as a show of sympathy or congratulations. Amazingly, the woman agreed that she had been remiss and said she would do it!

Twenty years later, the *Milwaukee Journal* printed a feature article with the headline: "African Violet Queen of Milwaukee Dies, Mourned by Thousands."

Granted, this is an exceptional story — or is it?

The African Violet lady was not propelled by a need to please, nor was her contribution dependent upon her giving money. Instead she gave freely of her time and talent.

For decades advertisers have convinced us that consuming and hoarding "stuff" will buy contentment. In buying their message we have missed the value of emptying ourselves of our gifts so that on the last day of our life we can proudly feel thoroughly used up.

Possibly the easiest way to care for another is to give someone the benefit of the doubt that you yearn for. Give them the smile you would love to receive. Help them in the ways you like to be helped. In general, stop thinking about yourself, drop your defenses and concentrate on caring for others without strings.

In *The Exquisite Risk*, poet and philosopher Mark Nepo speaks of the gift that comes with a life of simple caring:

> *There is nothing to accomplish. Only endless things to care for. Nothing to be mastered. Only an effort to lean into everything that is alive. Nothing to regret in what has brought us this far. Only gratitude that, as human beings...we are privileged to be guardians of our brief time on earth. Beyond the virtues of knowledge, the gift of such care is that it opens the well of being that makes life bearable.*[9]

With Nepo's words of wisdom, this book ends as your new life begins. I hope you have had long stretches of simmering between times of reading, for it is in silence that you determine *what* and *who* you intend to care about. And it is in solitude that you will realize it is up to you to finish what you were put on this earth to learn.

Your experience of loss has allowed you to know yourself better, but for me to assume that it has enhanced your life would be to romanticize despair. The facts, however, are undeniable: grief can ultimately bring out the best in you.

In the coming months catch yourself when you say "some people have all the luck!" Don't be so sure. The only life you can really know is your own.

Be grateful that fear is not a permanent state. It isn't. Nor is doubt. Each comes and goes.

Be aware of that you can become preoccupied with the life you think you deserve only to miss the one you have.

Be willing to nourish the part of you that wants to rally and *create a life that matters.*

And lastly, know that you can count on one thing: you are equipped to deal with it all.

> *This morning when I put on my shoes they seemed*
> *important, like the north and the south poles,*
> *and when I walked out and heard the noise of geese*
> *I looked up as if they were calling my name.*
> — Billy Collins, *The Last Man on Earth*

Notes

1. National Public Radio: 2012 Program: *Fresh Air* interview with Joan Rivers. http://www.wbur.org/npr/160398549/joan-rivers-hates-you-herself-and-everyone-else.
2. Bush, Ashley Davis (1997). *Transcending Loss*. New York: Berkeley Press. p. 210.
3. Seligman, Martin, Steen, Tracy, and Park, Nansook. Positive psychology progress: empirical validation of interventions. http://w.ebt.org/sites/www.ebt.org/files/empiricaldata.pdf.
4. Stanford University. *The psychology of happiness*. https://gsbapps.stanford.edu/cases/documents/M330.pdf. 8.1.10.
5. Adams, Rebecca (2009). What are friends for? A longer life. *New York Times*. 4.29 Health Section, p D1.http://www.nytimes.com/2009/04/21/health/21well.html.
6. Holt-Lunstad, J., Smith, T. B., and Layton, J. B. (2010). Social Relationships and Mortality Risk: A Meta-analytic Review. PLoS Med 7(7): e1000316. doi:10.1371/journal.pmed.1000316.
7. Dylan, Bob. Lyrics from "Alright, Ma (I'm Only Bleeding)."
8. O'Hanlon, William (2000). *Do One Thing Different*. New York: William Morrow.
9. Nepo, Mark (2006). *The Exquisite Risk*. New York: Three Rivers Press. p. 263.

About the Author

A PUBLISHED author, grief and loss counselor, and life transition coach, **Vicki Panagotacos, PhD, FT**, has lived in California since 1965 when she scraped together enough money for the train trip from the cold grey winters and humid summers of rural northwest Ohio. Her expectation that she would teach art, mother a large brood, and be the president of the PTA ended up to be far from reality.

Propelled by the unresolved grief in her own family, Vicki closed her award-winning design practice and returned to graduate school for a Masters in Transpersonal Psychology and a Doctorate in Thanatology. Her professional focus is on helping individuals maintain stability after the death of a loved one, and then partnering with them as they reclaim a vital lifestyle after the loss.

A veteran city girl, Vicki recently moved from the metropolitan San Francisco Bay Area to a rural area on the Monterey Peninsula. She maintains a private practice in Los Gatos, California, and continues her commitment to teaching and hospice work.

Ms. Panagotacos holds various professional certifications and is an ADEC Fellow. In addition to authoring *Gaining Traction: Starting Over after the Death of Your Life Partner*, Vicki writes for her blog, *TalkingGrief.com* and is the author of the chapter entitled "Defining and Envisioning Self in Techniques of Grief Therapy" in *Creative Practices for Counseling the Bereaved* (edited by Robert Niemeyer, 2012, Routledge), and the book *Effect of Multigenerational Family and Social Systems on Meaning-Making* (2010, Verlag).

Bibliography

Adams, Rebecca (2009). What are friends for? A longer life. *New York Times*. 4.29 Health Section, p. D1.http://www.nytimes.com/2009/04/21/health/21well.html.

American Psychological Association online: http://www.apa.org/monitor/2011/04/positive-psychology.aspx.

Andreas, Connie Rae (1994). *Core Transformation*. Boulder: Real People Press.

Andreas, Connie Rae (2009). Aligning Perceptual Positions: A new distinction in NLP *Journal of Consciousness Studies, Vol 16*, Numbers 10–12, 217–230(14).

Andreas, Stephen (2006). *Six Blind Elephants. Understanding Ourselves and Each Other. Vol 1*. Moab, UT: RealPeoplePress.

Aronson, J., Fried, C., and Good, C. (2002). Reducing the effects of stereotype threat on African American college students by shaping theories of intelligence. *Journal of Experimental Social Psychology*, 38, 113–125.

Attig, Tom (2010). *How We Grieve: Relearning the World*. New York: Oxford University Press.

Babauta, Leo. Zen Habits Post (4.12.13). A guide to practical contentment. http://zenhabits.net/contentment/.

Banikowsky, A. K. (1999). Strategies to enhance memory based on brain research. Retrieved from http://sc-boces.org/english/IMC/Focus/Memory _strategies2.pdf.

Beck, Martha (2002). *Finding Your Own North Star*. New York: Three Rivers Press.

Belk, R. W. (1988). Possessions and the extended self. *Journal of Consumer Research,* 15, 139–168.

Blackall, Sophia (2011). *Missed Connections: Love, Lost & Found*. New York: Workman Publishing.

Blackwell, I., Trzeniewski, K., and Dweck, C. (2007). Implicit theories of intelligence predict achievement across an adolescent transition: A longitudinal study and an intervention. *Child Development 78*,

246–263.

Bonanno G., Wortman, C., Lehman, D., et al. (2002). Resilience to loss and chronic grief: A prospective study from preloss to 18-months postloss. *Journal of Personality and Social Psychology*, Vol 83(5), 1150–1164.

Bonanno, G. A., Wortman, C. B., and Nesse, R. M. (2004). Prospective patterns of resilience and maladjustment during widowhood. Changing Lives of Older Couples (CLOC) study *Psychology and Aging*, 19(2), 260–271.

Bradshaw, John. Online: http://www.youtube.com/watch?v=2wzZi7BPJBI.

Brene Brown. http://www.ted.com/talks/brene _brown _on _ vulnerability.html.

Bridges, William (2001). *The Way of Transition: Embracing Life's Most Difficult Moments.* Da Capo Press.

Brooks, Mark. http://www.mcclatchydc.com/2008/07/16/v-print/44481/as-seniors-live-longer-they-find.html.

Brown, S., Bulanda, J.R., and Lee, G. (2005). The significance of nonmarital cohabitation: Marital status and mental health benefits among middle-aged and older adults. *J Gerontol B Psychol Sci Soc Sci (2005) 60 (1): S21–S29. doi:10.1093/geronb/60.1.S21.*

Browning, Dominique (2002). *Around the house and in the garden: a memoir of heartbreak, healing and home improvement.* New York: Scribner.

Bruner, Jerome. http://www.dundas.com/newsletters/2012/feb/index.html.

Bush, Ashley Davis (1997). *Transcending Loss.* New York: Berkeley Press.

Byrne, Rhonda (2006). *The Secret.* New York: Atria Books.

Carney, D. R., Cuddy, A. J. C., and Yap, A. J. (2010). Power posing: brief nonverbal displays affect neuroendocrine levels and risk tolerance. *Association of Psychological Science.* DOI:0.1177/0956797610383437.

Carr, Deborah (2004). The desire to date and remarry among older widows and widowers, *Journal of Marriage and Family.* 66, 1051–1068.

Chatauqua Institute: Conversation between Roger Roseblatt and Bishop Spong. http://fora.tv/2012/06/25/A _Conversation _Between _Roger _Rosenblatt _and Bishop _Spong.

Chatters, L. (2000). Religion and health: Public health research and practice. *Annual Review of Public Health,* Vol. 21: 335–367. doi: 0.1146/annurev.publhealth.21.1.335.

Chodron, Pema (2002). Shurnryu Suzuki Roshi quoted in *When things fall apart*. Boston: Shambala Publications.

Chopra, D. (1994). *Ageless body, timeless mind*. New York: Three Rivers Press.

Chopra, D., and Simon, D. (2002). *Grow younger, live longer*. New York: Three Rivers Press.

Clemmer, Jim (2003). *The Leader's Digest: Timeless Principles for Team and Organization Success*. Toronto: Ecw Press.

Colbert, Stephen. Playboy Interview with Stephen Colbert. Issue: Nov 2012. Online: http://www.colbertnewshub.com/2012/10/19/stephen-colbert-playboy-magzines-november-interview/.

Coles, Prophecy. (2011) *Uninvited Guests from Our Unremembered Past: an exploration of the unconscious transmission of trauma across the generations*. London: Karnac Books.

Conner, Marcia (2004). *Learn More Now*. Hoboken, NJ: John Wiley & Sons.

Conway, Susannah (2012). *This I Know: Notes on unraveling the heart*. Guilford: Globe Pequot Press.

Creswell, J. D., Irwin, M. R., et al. (2012). Mindfulness-based stress reduction training reduces loneliness and pro-inflammatory gene expression in older adults: A small randomized controlled trial. *Brain, Behavior, and Immunity.* doi:10.1016/j.bbi.2012.07.006.

Crowley, C., and Lodge, H. (2007). *Younger Next Year: Living Strong Until You're 80 and Beyond*. New York: Workman Publishing Company.

Dalai Lama (2001). *Ethics for the New Millennium*. New York: Riverhead Trade.

De La Rochefoucauld, Francois (1665–1678). Maxim 26 in *Reflections: or Sentences and Moral Maxims*.

Diener, Ed, and Biswas-Diener, Robert (2008). *Happiness*. Wiley-Blackwell; 1st edition.

Doidge, M.D., Norman (2007). *The Brain That Changes Itself*. New York: Penguin Books.

Doka, Kenneth (2002). How could God? In *Loss of the Assumptive World*, Ed., Jeffrey Kauffman. New York: Routledge.

Dwelk, C. (2008). Can Personality Be Changed? The role of beliefs in personality and change. *Association for Psychological Science, 17:6.*

Dwelk, C. (1999). *Self-theories: Their role in motivation, personality and development*. Philadelphia: Taylor and Francis/Psychology Press.

Dylan, Bob. Lyrics from "It's Alright, Ma (I'm Only Bleeding)."

Faulds, Donna (2002). Poem: "Allow in Go In and In." Berkeley:

Peaceable Kingdom.

Fisher, Helen (1994). *Anatomy of Love.* New York: Ballantine.

Frankl, Victor (1959). *Man's Search for Meaning.* New York: Meridian/ Plume.

Frankl, Victor (1988). *Will to Meaning,* New York: Beacon Press.

Fritz, Robert (2002). *Your Life as Art.* Robert Fritz Inc.

Fuller, R. C. (2001). *Spiritual but Not Religious.* New York: Oxford University Press.

Gaillard, R., Del Cul, A., and Naccache, L. et al. (2006). Nonconscious semantic processing of emotional words modulates conscious access. *Proc. Natl Acad, Sci. USA.* 103(19): 7524–9:7524–9. doi:10.1073/ pnas.0600584103.

Gallup, G., Jr. (2003). Americans' Spiritual Searches Turn Inward. Retrieved from http://www.gallup.com/poll/7759/americans- spiritual-searches-turn-inward.aspx.

Garfield, Charles (1984). *Athletes.* New York: Warner Books.

Gilbert, Dan. Online: http://www.ted.com/talks/dan _gilbert _asks _why _are _we _happy.html.

GlaxoSmithKline Online: http://www.gsksource.com/gskprm/en/US/ adirect/gskprm?cmd=ProductDetailPage&product _id=1336506912 652&featureKey=603462.

Goleman, Daniel (1985). *Vital Lies, Simple Truths.* New York: Simon & Schuster.

Gospel of Thomas. Retrieved from http://gnosis.org/naghamm/gosthom. html.

Goss, Tracy (1995). *The Last Word on Power.* New York: Crown Business.

Greenwald, A. G., Draine, S. C., and Abrams, R. L. (1996). Three cognitive markers of unconscious semantic activation. *Science* 273 (5282): 1699–702. doi:10.1126/science.

Guardian web site: http://www.guardian.co.uk/lifeandstyle/2012/sep/22/ dreamland-insomnia-sleep-cbt-drugs.

Hanson, Rick (2011). *Just One Thing.* Oakland: New Harbinger Publications.

Hirota, T., Wook, J., St. John, P., et al. (2012). Identification of small molecule activators of cryptochrome. *Science,* July 12 issue. doi: 10.1126/science.1223710.

Hollis, James (1996). *Swamplands of the Soul.* London: Inner City Books.

Hollis, James (2006). *Finding Meaning in the Second Half of Life.* New York: Gotham.

Holt-Lunstad, J., Smith, T. B., and Layton, J. B. (2010). Social

Relationships and Mortality Risk: A Meta-analytic Review. PLoS Med 7(7): e1000316. doi:10.1371/journal.pmed.1000316.

Huang, L. (2010). Powerful Postures Versus Powerful Roles: Which Is the Proximate Correlate of Thought and Behavior? *Psychological Science* January 2011 22: 95–102, first published on December 13, 2010 doi:10.1177/0956797610391912.

Huang, I.W., and Labroo, A. A. (2011). From Firm Muscles to Firm Willpower: Understanding the Role of Embodied Cognition in Self-Regulation. *Journal of Consumer Research*. Vol. 37, No. 6 (April 2011), 1046–1064. The University of Chicago Press. Article Stable http://www.jstor.org/stable/10.1086/657240.

Huffington Post. Why does writing make us smarter? http://www.huffingtonpost.com/2011/07/16/why-does-writing-make-us-n_900638.html.

Indrisano, R., and Paratore, J. R., (2005). *Learning to Write, Writing to Learn: Theory and Research in Practice* (No. 576–846). Newark, NJ: International Reading Association.

Jacobs, G. D., Pace-Schott, E. F., Stickhold, R., and Otto, M. W. (2004). Cognitive behavior therapy and pharmacology for insomnia. *Arch Intern Medicine* 164: 1888–96.

JAMA online. Time of day medicine dose is taken may boost its efficacy, cut toxicity. JAMA. 1996; 275:1 143–1 144. *Medical News & Perspectives.*

James, J. W., and Friedman, R. (2009). *The Grief Recovery Handbook.* 20th ed. New York: Harper Collins.

Johnson, M.D., Charles (1991). *Necessary Wisdom.* Berkeley, CA: Celestial Arts.

Kabat-Zinn, Jon (1990). *Full Catastrophe Living.* New York: Delta Bantam Dell.

Kalish, Nancy (1997). *Lost and found lovers: Facts and fantasies of rekindled romances.* New York: William Morrow.

Kaufman, Jeffrey (2002). *Loss of the Assumptive World: A Theory of Traumatic Loss (Series in Trauma and Loss).* Routledge.

Kay, Steve (2009). Biological Clock Chemical Offers Diabetes Treatment Hope. July 30. Online issue of *Science.* Retrieved from http://ucsdnews.ucsd.edu/pressrelease/discovery_of_chemical_that_affects_biological_clock_offers_new_way_to_treat.

Kegan, Robert, and Lahey, Lisa (2001). *How the Way We Talk Can Change the Way We Work.* San Francisco: Jossey-Bass/Wiley.

Kelley, M.M., and Chan, K. T. (2012): Assessing the role of attachment to God, meaning and religious coping as mediators in the grief experience. *Death Studies*, 36:3, 199–227.

Kiefer, M., and Brendel, D. (February 2006). Attentional modulation of unconscious "automatic" processes: evidence from event-related potentials in a masked priming paradigm. *Journal of Cognitive Neuroscience* 18 (2): 184–98. doi:10.1162/089892906775783688.

Kirkpatrick, Lee (1998). God as a substitute attachment figure: A longitudinal study of adult attachment style and religious change in college students. *Pers Soc Psychol Bull* vol. 24:9: pp 961–973. doi: 10.1177/0146167298249004.

Klass, D., Silverman, P. R., and Nickeman, S. (1996). *Continuing Bonds*. Washington, D.C: Taylor and Francis.

Kosminsky, Phyllis (2007). *Getting Back to Life When Grief Won't Heal*. New York: McGraw Hill.

Kross, E., Berman, M. G., Mischel, W., et al. (2011). Social rejection shares somatosensory representations with physical pain. *Proceedings of the National Academy of Sciences*. doi: 10.1073/pnas.1102693108.

Kundera, Milan (1999). *Immortality*. New York: Harper Perennial Modern Classics.

Landers, Casey (2010). Early childhood development. Unicef House. http://home1.gte.net/pulsar/Library _Ref/Biology/ECD/ECD%20 %202-6yrs.html.

Langer, E. J. (1989). *Mindfulness*. Reading, MA: Addison Wesley.

Langer, Helen (1998). *The Power of Mindful Thinking*, Cambridge, MA: DeCapo Press.

Lewis, C. S. (1961). *A Grief Observed*. New York: Bantam Books.

Luke, Helen M. (1988). *The Voice Within: Love and virtue in the age of the spirit*. New York: Crossroads Publishing.

Lyubomirsky, Sonja (2008). *The How of Happiness: a new approach to getting the life you want*. New York: Penguin Books.

MacKensie, Rosemary (date unknown). Poem: "Solstice." Source unknown.

Mangen, A. (2011). Digitizing literacy: reflections on the haptics of writing. *Advances In Haptics*. Retrieved from http://www.sciencedaily.com/releases/2011/01/110119095458.htm and http://www.uis.no/news/article29782-50.html.

Matchock, R., and Mordkoff, J.D. (2012). Chronotype and time-of-day influences on the alerting, orienting, and executive components of attention. *Research Gate* 192(2):189–198.

Matthews, G. (date unknown). Retrieved from http://www.dominican.

edu/dominicannews/study-backs-up-strategies-for-achieving-goals.

May, Rollo (1996). *The Meaning of Anxiety*. Rev. Ed. New York: W. W. Norton. Mayo Clinic Online: July, 2010. http://www.mayoclinic.com/health/fish-oil-supplements/AN01399.

Miller, Michael (1996). *Intimate Terrorism*. New York: W. W. Norton.

Minnini, Darlene (2006). *The Emotional Toolkit: Seven Power-Skills to Nail Your Bad Feelings*. New York: St. Martin's Griffin Press.

Mlodinow, Leonard (2012). *Subliminal: How Your Unconscious Mind Rules Your Behavior*. New York: Pantheon.

Moore-Ede, Martin (1994). *The Twenty-Four-Hour Society: Understanding Human Limits in a World That Never Stops*. Boston: Addison Wesley.

Moses, Anna. Online: http://www.gseart.com/Artists-Gallery/Moses-Anna-Mary-Robertson-Grandma/Moses-Anna-Mary-Robertson-Grandma-Biography.php.

Naccache, L., Gaillard, R., Adam, C., et al. (May 2005). A direct intracranial record of emotions evoked by subliminal words. *Proc. Natl. Acad. Sci. U.S.A.* 102 (21): 7713–7. doi:10.1073/pnas.0500542102.

National Public Radio: 2010 Program: Fresh Air interview with Father Gregory Boyle. http://www.npr.org/templates/story/story.php?storyId=127010471&ft=1&f=1008.

National Public Radio: 2012 Program: Fresh Air interview with Joan Rivers. http://www.wbur.org/npr/160398549/joan-rivers-hates-you-herself-and-everyone-else.

Neimeyer, R.A., Holland, J.M., et al. (2008). Meaning reconstruction in later life: Toward a cognitive-constructivist approach to grief therapy. In: Gallagher-Thompson, D., Steffan, A., Thompson, L., eds. Handbook of behavioral and cognitive therapies with older adults, 264–277. New York: Springer-Verlag.

Nepo, Mark (2006). *The Exquisite Risk*. New York: Three Rivers Press.

O'Hanlon, William (2000). *Do One Thing Different*. New York: William Morrow.

Oliver, Mary (1992). "Wild Geese" in *New and Selected Poems. Vol 1*. Boston: Beacon Press.

Palmer, Parker (2008). *A Hidden Wholeness: The Journey Toward an Undivided Life*. San Francisco: Jossey-Bass.

Palmer, Parker (1999). *An Active Life*. San Francisco: Jossey-Bass.

Petty, Richard (2009). Body posture affects confidence in your own thoughts. Research done at Ohio State University and also appeared in the October 2009 issue of the *European Journal of Social*

Psychology. http://researchnews.osu.edu/archive/posture.htm.

Prashant, Lyn (2002). *Degriefing: The Art of Transforming Grief.* http://www.degriefing.com/the-degriefing-manual.html.

Roberts, B.W., Walton, K.E., and Viechtbauer, W. (2006). Patterns of mean-level change in personality traits across the life course: A meta-analysis of longitudinal studies. *Psychological Bulletin, 132,* 1–25.

Rogers, Carl (1961). *On Becoming a Person.* London: Constable.

Rohn, Jim. www.JimRohn.com.

Rosenblatt, Roger (2012). *Kayak Morning: Reflections on Love, Grief, and Small Boats.* New York: Ecco.

Rosenblatt, Roger (2010). *Making Toast.* New York: Ecco.

Rossi, E. (1990). The eternal quest: Hidden rhythms of stress and healing in everyday life. *Psychological Perspectives,* 22, 6–23.

Rossi, E. (1993). The psychobiology of mind-body healing. Rev Ed. New York: W. W. Norton.

Rossi, E., and Lippincott, B. (1992). The wave nature of being: Ultradian rhythms and mind-body communication. In Lloyd, D, and Rossi, E. (Eds.) *Ultradian Rhythms in Life Processes: An Inquiry into Fundamental Principles of Chronobiology and Psychobiology.* 371–402. New York: Springer-Verlag.

Rupp, Joyce (1996). "Old maps no longer work" from *Dear Heart, Come Home: The Path of Midlife Spirituality.* New York: The Crossroad Publishing Company.

Schwartz, Richard C. (2008). You are the one you have been waiting for. Oak Park, IL: Center for Self Leadership.

Seligman, Martin, Steen, Tracy, and Park, Nansook. Positive psychology progress: empirical validation of interventions. *American Psychologist.* American Psychological Association 0003-066X/05. Vol. 60, No. 5, 410–421 DOI: 10.1037/0003-066X.60.5.410.

Sethi, Maneesh. Online: Blog: *Zen Habits* 3.26.13. https://mail.google.com/mail/?ui=2&ik=63d9df5091&view=pt&search=inbox&msg=13da879d448d3530.

Siegel, Dan (2010). *Mindsight: the new science of personal transformation.* New York: Bantam Books.

Smolensky, M.H., and D'alonzo, G. E. (1993). Medical Chronobiology: Concepts and Applications. *Am. J. Respir. Crit. Care Med.* 147:S2–S19

Specter, Herbert (1988). Neuroimmunolmodulation proceedings of the 1st international workshop, 188. Montreux, Switzerland: Fordonana Breach Science Publisher.

Stanford University. The psychology of happiness. https://gsbapps.

stanford.edu/cases/documents/M330.pdf. 8.1.10.

Striebe, G. F., and Schneider, C. J., (1971). Retirement in American society: Impact and process. Ithaca, NY.: Cornell University Press.

Stroebe, M., and Schut, H. (1999). The dual process model of coping with bereavement: rationale and description. *Death Studies,* Vol 23:3.

Tedeschi, R., and Calhoun, L. (2004). Posttraumatic growth: Conceptual foundations and empirical evidence. *Psychological Inquiry*, 15:1, 1–18.

Tharp, Twyla (2005). *The Creative Habit*. New York: Simon & Schuster.

The Pacific Institute Investment in Excellence Seminar. http://www.thepacificinstitute.us/v2/

Theole, Sue Patton (2011). *The Courage to Be a Stepmom: Finding Your Place Without Losing Yourself.* E-Book/Amazon.

Touch: The Forgotten Sense (2001). Film produced by Max Films. http://www.imdb.com/title/tt0903652/.

Trungpa, Chogyam (1978). *Shambhala: The Sacred Path of the Warrior.* Boston: Shambhala Publications.

UC-Fullerton online article (2006). http://commfaculty.fullerton.edu/lester/writing/wiscomtheory.html.

Viorst, Judith (1998). *Necessary Losses*. New York: Free Press.

Wall Street Journal. (2012). The peak time for everything; *Personal Journ Sec* 9.26.12.

Watermark: A Poet's Notebook. http://www.sbpoet.com/2004/04/already_broken _.html.

Wieth, M. B. and Zacks, R. T. (2011). Time-of-day effects on problem solving: When the non-optimal is optimal. *Thinking & Reasoning*, 17, 387–401.

Wolpe, David (2009). *Why Faith Matters*. San Francisco: HarperOne.

Wortman, C.B., and Boerner, K. (2007). In H.S. Friedman and R.C. Silver (Eds.), *Foundations of Healthy Psych.* pp. 285–324. New York: Oxford University Press.

Yalom, Irwin (2009). *Staring at the Sun: Overcoming the Terror of Death.* San Francisco: Jossey-Bass.

Yapko, Michael (2012). *Trancework: An introduction to the Practice of Clinical Hypnosis.* 4th Ed. New York: Routledge.

Made in the USA
San Bernardino, CA
17 March 2015